BOOK TWO

FUN FOR FAMILY NIGHT

BOOK TWO

FUN FOR FAMILY NIGHT

Easy to Prepare
Lessons · Activities · Stories · Games
And other ideas
to make learning fun

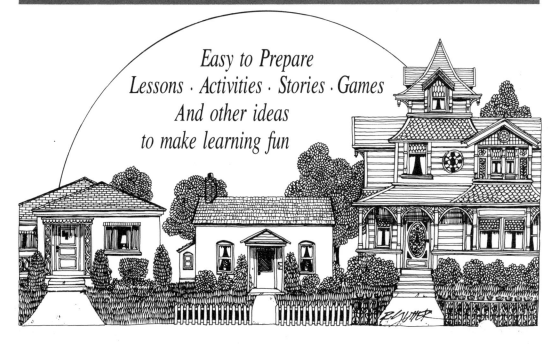

Allan K. Burgess   Max H. Molgard

Bookcraft

Salt Lake City, Utah

Library of Congress Catalog Card Number: 91–77881

ISBN 0–88494–817–X

First Printing, 1992

Printed in the United States of America

Contents

RESOURCES

Introduction

What can parents do to get their children excited and involved in gospel learning? How can they make family home evenings a time of closeness and bonding instead of contention? Where can they go to quickly get exciting ideas and activities? These and similar concerns led to the compilation of this series of family night books containing material that is quick and easy to prepare, varied in its content, and appealing to a wide range of ages. It is hoped that the material is also helpful in bringing family members closer together.

This book (the second in the series) contains lessons and activities that focus on Church history, the Doctrine and Covenants, family relationships, and many other gospel topics. This material can help you teach the gospel to your family, and it can provide you with the tools for having a successful family night, if you will do your part by praying, preparing, and building positive patterns. Here are some suggestions:

1. *Choose a lesson.* You know your family better than anyone else does, so make your choice based on their time, habits, needs, and interests. You can go through the lessons in the order they appear in the book (they have been placed so as to provide variety from week to week), or you can choose a lesson out of order if you find one that is just right for a particular event or person or need.

2. *Read over the lesson you have chosen.* This will give you a general sense of the lesson's focus and of the time and materials required.

3. *Prepare the materials you'll need.* Each lesson starts with a section called "Advance Preparation." The preparation is usually quick and simple, but it will work even better if you keep close at hand certain supplies. Make a place to keep the things you use most frequently for family night. You could use a box, a file, a drawer, or a shelf to keep items such as the following:

- Copies of the scriptures
- Marking pencils
- Paper
- Pens and pencils

- Lesson book
- Masking tape
- Envelopes
- Scissors

This will also become a place to save the materials that you prepare in each lesson so you can use them again. In this book the pages containing game pieces and other activity items have "cut lines" along the left-hand margin. Use scissors or an X-acto® knife to remove these pages, and, to preserve the items, you may want to photocopy and laminate them.

4. *Use the "Resources" section.* In some lessons the "Advance Preparation" section will refer you to a chapter in the "Resources" section at the back of the book. The material in this section can be used in conjunction with the lessons in this book, or it can be used to develop or supplement your own family night lesson or activity.

5. *Do it!* Conduct your family nights in your own way. Adapt the lessons and activities so they'll be comfortable for you and your family. For example, if your family is small, adapt directions that say, "Divide into four teams"; two teams might work better for you. If you have family members who do not read yet, adapt by making sure they have partners who can read to them when necessary. If you have family members who are ready for deeper

discussions, allow time for that. Above all, keep trying. As you improve with practice, your family night can become a fun time for learning about the gospel of Jesus Christ and for learning to love each other.

Lessons

and

Activities

1

Heroes

Advance Preparation

1. Paper and pencil or pen for each family member.
2. Cut out Bingo sheets and twenty-four blank strips found at the end of this lesson.
3. Collect markers for Bingo game, about twenty for each person or each pair. You could use buttons, beans, coins, popcorn, paper cutouts, etc.
4. Bowl or sack.

Lesson Background

The purpose of this lesson is to help your family understand that having religious heroes in our lives can help us become better. As we study Church history and the scriptures there are many people we can view as heroes to better our lives.

Activity

1. Divide the family into pairs, with older and younger members paired together. Give each pair a pencil and three pieces of paper.
2. Explain to them that you will read a word and they should write down the name of a person they think of when they hear the word.
3. Read the first word from this list:

Tall	Strong	Righteous	Smart
Fun	Little	Kind	Villain
Handsome	Cute	Famous	Hero

Allow time for each pair to write down a name. Then ask a member of each team in turn to read his or her team's answer aloud. A team receives five points if no other team has the same answer. If another team has the same answer they receive no points.

4. Continue play until all of the words have been used.
5. After all the words have been used have each team draw a picture of what they think a villain looks like and then a picture of what they think a hero looks like. Under each picture have them write a definition of what a villain is and what a hero is. After they are finished have each team share their picture and definition with the rest of the family.

Application

Explain to the family that it is important for all of us to have heroes. Heroes are people we look up to and who help us make our lives better by their good example. Many great people in the history of the Church can be considered heroes. Parents could share the

3

names of some people they consider to be heroes and how those people have helped them to become better persons. Others in the family could also do this.

Conclude by asking family members who they would consider to be the greatest villain of all time and why. Explain that Satan is the greatest villain of all time. Discuss reasons. For instance, Satan rebelled and continues to rebel against God. He thinks mainly of himself and wants to have power over everyone. Then ask the family who the greatest hero of all time is and why. Explain that Heavenly Father and Jesus are the greatest heroes of all time. Their chief interest is our eternal happiness.

Game: Hero Bingo

1. Ask family members to name twenty-four people who could be considered heroes. Write them down on the twenty-four blank strips.

2. Have family members decide whether they want to play as individuals or as pairs. Give each person (or pair) one Bingo sheet.

3. Each person or pair writes the names of the heroes in the squares of the Bingo sheet, in random order.

4. Put the twenty-four strips with the heroes' names written on them into a bowl or sack.

5. Give each individual or pair a set of markers.

6. Begin by drawing a name from the bowl and reading it. (For a more difficult version, give clues about the person rather than reading the name.) Each person or pair then places a marker on the square naming the correct person. The first person to get five markers in a row and yell "Bingo" wins. You might want to have some kind of reward for the winner of each game.

7. After someone has won, you may play again. Clear the cards of markers, put all the names back into the bowl, and begin again.

Hero Bingo

		FREE		

Hero Bingo

		FREE		

Hero Bingo

		FREE		

Hero Bingo

		FREE		

Hero Bingo

		FREE		

Hero Bingo

		FREE		

i

2

Search These Commandments
D & C 1:37–38

Advance Preparation

1. A personal copy of the Doctrine and Covenants for each family member. (Younger children can be assisted in finding and marking scriptures even if they cannot yet read. Used copies can sometimes be obtained for younger children.)
2. Red pencils or pens for each family member.
3. Cut out the enlarged drawing of figure 1 found at the end of this lesson.
4. Read Doctrine and Covenants 1:37–38.

Activity: How Many Squares?

Figure 1

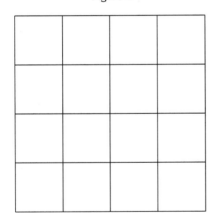

Figure 2

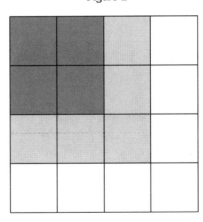

Hold up the enlarged drawing of figure 1 and ask family members how many squares they see. It is possible to find thirty squares. Many people, however, see only sixteen squares, and very few identify all thirty. In order to find all thirty squares a person would need to take the time to really search. (Figure 2 identifies some of the squares that may be missed unless we take the time to search carefully.)

The scriptures are much the same way. The Lord does not ask us merely to read the scriptures; he uses such words as *study, seek,* and *diligently search.* There is a great difference between reading and searching. The following story illustrates the difference between just looking and really searching.

Story

A young six-year-old boy had somehow wandered away from his handcart company during a storm and was lost. When the parents, Robert and Ann Parker, realized their boy

13

was missing, they were frantic. All of the men in the company spent the next two days searching for the lost boy. He was not found, and the decision was made that, because of the approaching winter, the handcart train would need to continue on the next morning.

The father decided to send his wife and other children ahead with their handcart, and he would stay behind to search back down the trail until he found their son—dead or alive. Ann Parker pinned a bright red shawl around her husband's thin shoulders and told him to wrap their son in it if he were found dead. If the father found their boy alive, he was to wave the shawl as a signal as soon as he could be seen by her and the other children.

The handcarts pulled out the next morning with Ann and her children struggling with the heavy load. Robert retraced the miles of trail, calling, searching, and praying for his six-year-old son. Surely he didn't just casually look behind a few trees or leisurely walk back along the trail. He must have vigorously investigated every thicket, clump of trees, and gully or wash that he came to. Finally, he found his son. With the help of God and an old woods-man and the woodsman's wife, his son had been kept alive. The woodsman had found the boy almost dead from fright and exposure and, with his wife, had nursed him back to health.

You can imagine how happy the father must have been to find his son still alive and how he must have anticipated bringing the boy back to his mother and family again. Undoubtedly he made quick time back up the trail with his precious son.

Meanwhile, the mother had been constantly looking back down the trail. Every minute of sunlight was spent in searching the horizon for a glimpse of her husband and, she hoped, the signal of the red shawl. After three days of diligent watching, she saw a figure in the distance. As she strained her eyes to see more clearly, she saw the sun glint off the red shawl. As a feeling of relief and joy swept over her, she finally gave in to her exhausted body and slumped into unconsciousness upon the trail. When she recovered her strength, her family was whole again. (See LeRoy R. Hafen and Ann W. Hafen, *Handcarts to Zion* [Glendale, California: The Arthur H. Clark Company, 1960], pp. 61, 63–64.)

Application

Too often we simply browse or skim as we read the scriptures. If we would search the scriptures with the same vigor that Robert hunted for his son, the scriptures would come alive to us.

Ask the following question: What should we be searching for when we study the scriptures? (Possible answers: solutions to personal problems, or insights that will help us present a lesson. Maybe the most important reason for searching the scriptures is to find out what God wants us to do so we can live a better life and be happier.)

Scripture

Read Doctrine & Covenants 1:37–38 aloud and have each family member mark these verses in his or her own copy of the scriptures. "Search the Comm." could be written in the margin. (If there isn't enough room in the margin, draw an asterisk or star in the margin. Then draw an asterisk at the top or bottom of the page and write "37" next to it and "Search the Comm." [Example: *37 Search the Comm.] When you see the asterisk next to verse 37 it will tell you that you have written something concerning that verse at the top or bottom of the page. Follow this same approach any time there is not enough room to write in the margin.)

Ask the following questions:

1. What should we search for when studying the scriptures? (This will be a review of the principle taught above.)

2. How many promises of God will be fulfilled? (All of them.)

14

3. What are some things God has promised? (He will forgive us when we repent; we will be resurrected; we can be together as families; tithe payers will be blessed; etc.)

4. The scripture says, "By mine own voice or by the voice of my servants, it is the same." What does this mean, and who are some of God's servants included in this statement? (Included in this statement when they are speaking by the power of the Spirit are prophets, Apostles, bishops, stake presidents, Relief Society presidents, etc.) See Doctrine & Covenants 68:3–4 for added insight.

Game: How Well Do You Know the Prophets?

This game can be played as teams or as individuals. As with all activities and games in this book, young children can be matched with older family members so that all ages can participate.

Tell the family that there have been thirteen latter-day Presidents of the Church who have all given us the word of God. Read each of the following questions about these prophets along with the three possible answers for each. A team or individual will receive a point for choosing a correct answer. (Correct answers are in bold italic print.)

An extra dimension could be added to the game by having each person or team also risk a point on whether or not they think the person or team on their right will answer the question correctly. If the person or team risking a point predicts correctly, they receive another point; if they predict incorrectly, they lose a point.

1. Which President held the office of Apostle longer than any other?
   a. Brigham Young   b. ***David O. McKay***   c. Joseph Fielding Smith

2. Which of the following prophets was the oldest of eleven children who all served full-time missions?
   a. David O. McKay   b. ***Ezra Taft Benson***   c. Harold B. Lee

3. Who received the revelation allowing all worthy male members to be ordained to the priesthood?
   a. ***Spencer W. Kimball***   b. Harold B. Lee
   c. Joseph Fielding Smith

4. Who took lonely people for car rides on a regular basis?
   a. George Albert Smith   b. Spencer W. Kimball   c. ***Heber J. Grant***

5. How did Joseph Fielding Smith gain three hundred extra hours per year?
   a. Got up earlier   b. ***Worked during noon hour***
   c. Quit watching television

6. Which President was known for his many accidents as a youth?
   a. Spencer W. Kimball   b. ***Wilford Woodruff***   c. Joseph F. Smith

7. Who was rebaptized because he was first baptized in a bathtub?
   a. David O. McKay   b. Ezra Taft Benson
   c. ***Spencer W. Kimball***

8. Who was the only Church President born outside of the United States?
   a. ***John Taylor***   b. Heber J. Grant   c. Brigham Young

15

9. As a young man, which President sang with the Tabernacle Choir?
   a. David O. McKay   b. ***Joseph Fielding Smith***
   c. Harold B. Lee

10. Which president played four musical instruments?
    a. Spencer W. Kimball   b. ***Harold B. Lee***   c. Lorenzo Snow

11. What did Brigham Young have installed in the Salt Lake Theatre?
    a. Bed   b. Reading lamp   c. ***Rocking chair***

12. What were Brigham Young's false teeth made of?
    a. Wood   b. Ivory   c. ***Porcelain and gold***

13. Who led the Church longer than any other President?
    a. ***Brigham Young***   b. Spencer W. Kimball   c. John Taylor

14. Which President enjoyed people so much that he sometimes traveled with over one hundred people?
    a. Joseph Smith   b. ***Brigham Young***   c. Spencer W. Kimball

15. Which President of the Church was the shortest?
    a. Spencer W. Kimball   b. Wilford Woodruff   c. ***Lorenzo Snow***

3

Learning the Order of the Presidents of the Church

Advance Preparation

1. Obtain a large folder and smaller envelopes in which to keep the game squares when family night is over.
2. Cut out the Presidents of the Church picture cards found at the end of this lesson.
3. Label an envelope "Presidents of the Church."
4. Cut out the numbered squares found at the end of this lesson. Only fourteen squares are used in this game; the remaining squares will be used in other games.
5. Label an envelope "Numbered Squares."

Activity

Working together as a family, learn the Presidents of the Church in order.

1. Joseph Smith
2. Brigham Young
3. John Taylor
4. Wilford Woodruff
5. Lorenzo Snow
6. Joseph F. Smith
7. Heber J. Grant
8. George Albert Smith
9. David O. McKay
10. Joseph Fielding Smith
11. Harold B. Lee
12. Spencer W. Kimball
13. Ezra Taft Benson

To help you as a family in learning and reviewing the Presidents, cut out the cards showing the Presidents of the Church. You will also need an envelope labeled "Presidents of the Church" in which to put the cards when you are done. These cards will be used in future lessons as a review. Use the four cards with all the Presidents listed on them to learn the order in which they served. The Follow the Prophets card is used as a wild card in some of the review games. When the family members feel they have learned the Presidents' names and the order in which they served, they may play the following games as a fun review.

Every Other One

1. Divide the family into two teams.

2. Begin with one of the people on a team naming Joseph Smith. A person on the other team should then name Brigham Young. Each team has five seconds to name the right President.

3. Players alternate back and forth, naming the Presidents in order, until one of the teams misses or all of the Presidents have been named.

4. Everyone on a team must take his or her turn in trying to name a President before someone can take another turn.

5. Several rounds of this game could be played. Each time a new round begins, start with someone different than the person who started the previous round.

6.   Another version of this game is to have one family member challenge another family member and just go back and forth between the two.

Who's the Fastest?

Have a contest to see who can name the Presidents in order the fastest. Time each person as he names the Presidents. Write down each person's fastest time. Each person could try to break his or her previous best time. You could also have a family record. Each week at the beginning or end of family night you could see if anyone would like to try to break the record.

Find It in Order

1.   Divide the family into two teams.
2.   Place the Follow the Prophets card and the cards for the Presidents of the Church face down in two rows of seven on the floor or table. Then cover the cards, using the numbered squares 1–14.
3.   One team begins by selecting one of the numbers and then picking up both the number card and the President card and turning it over so the President card is showing. If the President is Joseph Smith the team gets to keep the card. If it is any other President, a team member turns it back over so the number is showing. The other team then takes a turn trying to find the Joseph Smith card.
4.   After the Joseph Smith card is found, the teams then take turns trying to find the next President, Brigham Young. The first team to find the Brigham Young card then keeps it, and play rotates to the other team.
5.   Play continues until all the Presidents have been uncovered in order. The team with the most cards wins.
6.   The Follow the Prophets card is a wild card. The first team to uncover it gets to keep it.

Note: Be sure to save the Presidents of the Church cards in an envelope labeled "Presidents of the Church" and the numbered squares in another envelope labeled "Numbered Squares," so that these game pieces can be used again in other lessons. Put these envelopes in a family night folder when the lesson is over so they will not be misplaced.

Joseph Smith

Joseph Smith

Brigham Young

Brigham Young

John Taylor

John Taylor

Wilford Woodruff

Wilford Woodruff

Lorenzo Snow

Lorenzo Snow

Joseph F. Smith

Joseph F. Smith

Heber J. Grant

Heber J. Grant

George Albert Smith

George Albert Smith

David O. McKay

David O. McKay

Joseph Fielding Smith

Joseph Fielding Smith

Harold B. Lee

Harold B. Lee

Spencer W. Kimball

Spencer W. Kimball

Ezra Taft Benson

Ezra Taft Benson

Follow the Prophets

Follow the Prophets

1. Joseph Smith
2. Brigham Young
3. John Taylor
4. Wilford Woodruff
5. Lorenzo Snow
6. Joseph F. Smith
7. Heber J. Grant
8. George Albert Smith
9. David O. McKay
10. Joseph Fielding Smith
11. Harold B. Lee
12. Spencer W. Kimball
13. Ezra Taft Benson

1. Joseph Smith
2. Brigham Young
3. John Taylor
4. Wilford Woodruff
5. Lorenzo Snow
6. Joseph F. Smith
7. Heber J. Grant
8. George Albert Smith
9. David O. McKay
10. Joseph Fielding Smith
11. Harold B. Lee
12. Spencer W. Kimball
13. Ezra Taft Benson

1. Joseph Smith
2. Brigham Young
3. John Taylor
4. Wilford Woodruff
5. Lorenzo Snow
6. Joseph F. Smith
7. Heber J. Grant
8. George Albert Smith
9. David O. McKay
10. Joseph Fielding Smith
11. Harold B. Lee
12. Spencer W. Kimball
13. Ezra Taft Benson

1. Joseph Smith
2. Brigham Young
3. John Taylor
4. Wilford Woodruff
5. Lorenzo Snow
6. Joseph F. Smith
7. Heber J. Grant
8. George Albert Smith
9. David O. McKay
10. Joseph Fielding Smith
11. Harold B. Lee
12. Spencer W. Kimball
13. Ezra Taft Benson

1	2	3
4	5	6
7	8	9

10	11	12
13	14	15
16	17	18

4

The First Vision

Advance Preparation

1. Paper and pencils for each family member (those who can't write yet may be teamed with older family members).
2. Personal scriptures and marking pencils.
3. Cut out the mazes found at the end of this lesson.
4. Cut out the squares for the Finding the Truth game found at the end of this lesson.
5. Numbered squares (used in lesson 3).

Activity: Clue

This activity can be done as individuals or as teams. Family members try to guess which important event you are thinking of by listening carefully to the clues (listed below) and writing down, *after each clue,* what they think the event is. No answers are given aloud until all of the clues have been given. When all of the clues have been given, the winner is the person who wrote down the correct answer the earliest and did not change his or her answer with future clues. The clues are difficult at first but get progressively easier. (The event is the First Vision.)

1. It is one of the most important events that has ever taken place.
2. It did not happen in a building.
3. It took great faith and effort.
4. The Bible played a part in this event.
5. It involved prayer.
6. It has something to do with Joseph Smith.
7. Joseph Smith was fourteen years old at the time.
8. Jesus and Heavenly Father were involved.
9. This event is called the First _____.

Scripture or Story

If the members of your family are older, have them turn to Joseph Smith—History 1:5, 10–19 in the Pearl of Great Price. Read and mark the scriptures together.

If you have young children you may want to read them the following simplified version of the scriptural account and then mark a few of the verses in their scriptures.

When Joseph Smith was fourteen years old, everyone seemed to be wondering which church to go to. Some of his family members joined the Presbyterian church, but Joseph continued to visit several churches. He wondered if there was a true Church and how he could know which one it was. As he went to the different churches, many of them said that they were true, and some of them even taught that it didn't matter which church you went to as long as you went to one of them.

Joseph became very confused. He didn't know who to trust. Finally, he decided that only God could help him find the true Church. He kept thinking and searching for an answer.

One day, as he was reading the Bible, he read a scripture that told him that if he prayed with real faith, he could get his questions answered. Joseph was excited. He went to a place in the forest where it was quiet and where he knew he could be completely alone. He knelt down, bowed his head, closed his eyes, and started to pray aloud. Satan tried to stop him. He knew how important Joseph's prayer was, and he tried to frighten and discourage him. But Joseph continued to pray.

Then a great and marvelous thing happened—Heavenly Father and Jesus appeared to Joseph Smith. Joseph asked them which church he should join and was told to join none of them. He found out that the true gospel would be made known to him at a future time.

Application

When we have questions, we can pray and we will receive answers also. Our prayers are answered in many different ways. Sometimes we will ask if something is right, and we will get a good feeling inside that tells us that it is. Other times we feel the Holy Ghost tell us what to do. Sometimes we will read the answer in the scriptures, or Heavenly Father will send us help through another person. We don't always get the answer right away, but if we pray in faith, Heavenly Father will always answer our prayers.

Activity: Maze

Give a maze sheet to each person or group of people. Tell them that you are going to read some sentences, some true and some false. If they think the sentence is true, family members should go *right* on the maze sheet. If they think the sentence is false, they should go *left*. If they respond correctly to all ten sentences, they will get through the maze.

1. Joseph was fourteen years old when he prayed in the woods. (True.)
2. Joseph's family didn't care about religion. (False.)
3. Joseph looked in the Book of Mormon for help. (False.)
4. Joseph read an important scripture in the Bible. (True.)
5. Joseph went to a grove of trees to pray. (True.)
6. Satan wants good things to happen. (False.)
7. Heavenly Father has more power than Satan. (True.)
8. When Joseph prayed, he saw only one person. (False.)
9. Joseph was told to join any church he wanted to. (False.)
10. Prayers are not always answered right away. (True.)

Game: Finding the Truth

This game is very simple, but people of all ages seem to have a lot of fun with it. Cut out the nine squares that make up the game. Eight of the squares name ways that we can find the truth, and on the ninth square is the word *Truth*.

Mix up the squares and place them face down on the floor or table in three rows of three. Cover these squares with numbered squares 1 through 9 (the numbered squares are from lesson 3; their use here will ensure that no one can see any of the words on the Finding the Truth squares).

The idea of the game is to see how many squares a family member has to turn over before he or she can find the truth. As soon as one person finds the truth square, the squares are reshuffled and placed down for the next family member. Each player may take several turns if time permits.

Another variation of play is to have family members take turns trying to uncover the truth square. Each person turns over only one square, then the next person turns over a square, until the word *Truth* is discovered.

A third variation is to divide the family into teams. Players from opposing teams alternate in turning over a square each. Points are scored each time one of the teams uncovers the truth square.

Note: Be sure to save the truth squares in an envelope labeled "Finding the Truth Game" so that the game pieces can be used again in other lessons. Return numbers 1 through 9 to the "Numbered Squares" envelope and put both envelopes in your family night folder so they will not be misplaced.

Start

Start

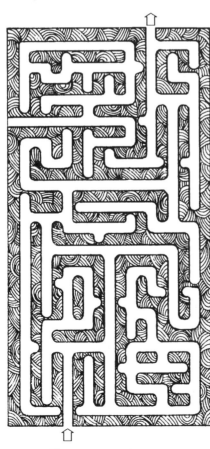

Start

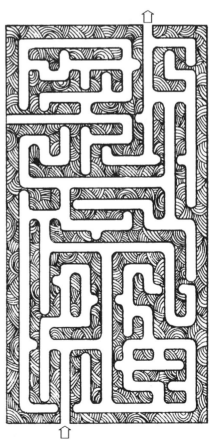

Start

Scriptures	**Prayer**	**Prophets**
Conference	**Parents**	**Holy Ghost**
Teachers	**Blessings**	**Truth**

5

Marking Key Scriptures

Advance Preparation

1. Personal scriptures and marking pencils.
2. Cut out the bookmarks found at the end of this lesson.
3. Label three envelopes "Key Scripture Picture Cards," "Key Scripture Statement Cards," and "Key Scripture Reference Cards."
4. Cut out picture, statement, and reference cards found at the end of this lesson. Together these three sets of cards make up your Key Scripture cards. Keep them in their respective envelopes for future use.

Activity

To help the family become familiar with some important scriptures in the Doctrine and Covenants, key scriptures from this sacred volume will be introduced throughout the lessons in this book. This lesson is a time for the family to mark these key scriptures. A bookmark for each family member has been provided at the end of the lesson. These may be cut out and placed in each person's copy of the Doctrine and Covenants for future reference. Next to the scripture references on the bookmark are pictures that can help family members remember what the particular scripture is about. Matching pictures could be drawn in a person's copy of the Doctrine and Covenants close to the corresponding scriptures (for example, in the margin, or at the top or bottom of the page). These pictures will be especially helpful for those children who cannot yet read. They will be able to participate in finding scriptures with the rest of the family by just looking for the pictures.

The other two items found on the bookmark are scripture references and short key statements. The key statement is another quick reminder of what the scripture is about. This could also be written in a person's copy of the Doctrine and Covenants close to the scripture.

Using your personal copies of the scriptures, as a family mark each scripture listed on the bookmark (for D&C 89, you may want to simply circle the section number), and in the margin write the key statement and/or draw the scripture picture.

Review

Review the scriptures by using the Key Scripture picture cards. Place all of the picture cards face down on the floor or table. Turn the top card over and have everyone find the matching scripture in his or her copy of the Doctrine and Covenants. After all family members have found the scripture, turn over another card. Continue this until all of the cards have been turned over. Family members can use their bookmarks if needed.

Note on Teaching Young Children about Scriptures

Even young children can feel the importance of the scriptures. This is particularly true if parents have set the example of carrying and reading their scriptures. Little ones want to be "just like Mommy and Daddy." You can take advantage of this trait by buying them inexpensive or used versions of the scriptures for them to learn to love.

Even before they can read, you can teach them many things as they use their scriptures. You can start by acquainting them with the standard works. This is done by placing the separate copies of the standard works in a row in front of your child. As you say "Bible" or "Book of Mormon" or name one of the other books, help the child learn to put his or her hand on the correct book. If you follow up by showing your approval, they will perfect this skill in no time.

The next step is to ask or talk about something pertaining to a specific book and have the child put his or her hand on the correct book. For example, you could ask, "Which book tells about Jesus being born?" or "Which book tells about Jesus coming to America?"

Games

This would be a good time to review the Presidents of the Church in order. Look up the rules for the High-Low game in the chapter "Games for Many Occasions."

Also, during this and future family nights, you may want to take advantage of the many activities and games found in the chapter "Key Scripture Ideas." These activities and games will help family members to review key scriptures from the Doctrine and Covenants that are introduced in various lessons in this book. In fact, after having gone through all the lessons that introduce the key scriptures, you may want to devote an entire family night to reviewing them by using activities and games from the chapter "Key Scripture Ideas."

Doctrine and Covenants

 D&C 1:37–38 — Search the Scriptures

 D&C 8:2–3 — Spirit of Revelation

 D&C 10:5 — Pray Always

 D&C 18:10, 15–16 — Great Shall Be Your Joy

 D&C 20:77, 79 — Sacrament Prayers

 D&C 58:42–43 — Repentance

 D&C 59:9–10 — Sabbath Day Holy

 D&C 61:36 — Be of Good Cheer

 D&C 64:9–11 — Forgive One Another

 D&C 89 — Word of Wisdom

Doctrine and Covenants

 D&C 1:37–38 — Search the Scriptures

 D&C 8:2–3 — Spirit of Revelation

 D&C 10:5 — Pray Always

 D&C 18:10, 15–16 — Great Shall Be Your Joy

 D&C 20:77, 79 — Sacrament Prayers

 D&C 58:42–43 — Repentance

 D&C 59:9–10 — Sabbath Day Holy

 D&C 61:36 — Be of Good Cheer

 D&C 64:9–11 — Forgive One Another

 D&C 89 — Word of Wisdom

Doctrine and Covenants

 D&C 1:37–38 — Search the Scriptures

 D&C 8:2–3 — Spirit of Revelation

 D&C 10:5 — Pray Always

 D&C 18:10, 15–16 — Great Shall Be Your Joy

 D&C 20:77, 79 — Sacrament Prayers

 D&C 58:42–43 — Repentance

 D&C 59:9–10 — Sabbath Day Holy

 D&C 61:36 — Be of Good Cheer

 D&C 64:9–11 — Forgive One Another

 D&C 89 — Word of Wisdom

Doctrine and Covenants

 D&C 1:37–38 — Search the Scriptures

 D&C 8:2–3 — Spirit of Revelation

 D&C 10:5 — Pray Always

 D&C 18:10, 15–16 — Great Shall Be Your Joy

 D&C 20:77, 79 — Sacrament Prayers

 D&C 58:42–43 — Repentance

 D&C 59:9–10 — Sabbath Day Holy

 D&C 61:36 — Be of Good Cheer

 D&C 64:9–11 — Forgive One Another

D&C 89 — Word of Wisdom

Doctrine and Covenants

 D&C 1:37–38 — Search the Scriptures

 D&C 8:2–3 — Spirit of Revelation

 D&C 10:5 — Pray Always

 D&C 18:10, 15–16 — Great Shall Be Your Joy

 D&C 20:77, 79 — Sacrament Prayers

 D&C 58:42–43 — Repentance

 D&C 59:9–10 — Sabbath Day Holy

 D&C 61:36 — Be of Good Cheer

 D&C 64:9–11 — Forgive One Another

 D&C 89 — Word of Wisdom

Doctrine and Covenants

 D&C 1:37–38 — Search the Scriptures

 D&C 8:2–3 — Spirit of Revelation

 D&C 10:5 — Pray Always

 D&C 18:10, 15–16 — Great Shall Be Your Joy

 D&C 20:77, 79 — Sacrament Prayers

 D&C 58:42–43 — Repentance

 D&C 59:9–10 — Sabbath Day Holy

 D&C 61:36 — Be of Good Cheer

 D&C 64:9–11 — Forgive One Another

 D&C 89 — Word of Wisdom

Doctrine and Covenants

 D&C 1:37–38 — Search the Scriptures

 D&C 8:2–3 — Spirit of Revelation

 D&C 10:5 — Pray Always

 D&C 18:10, 15–16 — Great Shall Be Your Joy

 D&C 20:77, 79 — Sacrament Prayers

 D&C 58:42–43 — Repentance

 D&C 59:9–10 — Sabbath Day Holy

 D&C 61:36 — Be of Good Cheer

 D&C 64:9–11 — Forgive One Another

 D&C 89 — Word of Wisdom

Doctrine and Covenants

 D&C 1:37–38 — Search the Scriptures

 D&C 8:2–3 — Spirit of Revelation

 D&C 10:5 — Pray Always

 D&C 18:10, 15–16 — Great Shall Be Your Joy

 D&C 20:77, 79 — Sacrament Prayers

 D&C 58:42–43 — Repentance

 D&C 59:9–10 — Sabbath Day Holy

 D&C 61:36 — Be of Good Cheer

 D&C 64:9–11 — Forgive One Another

D&C 89 — Word of Wisdom

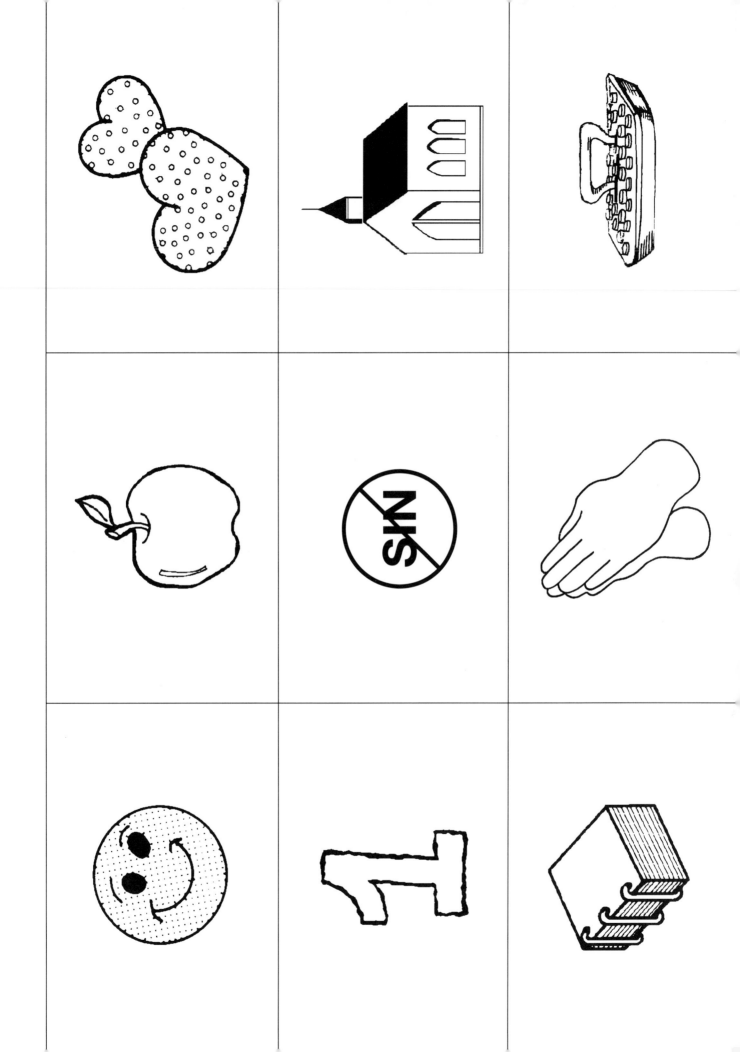

	Sabbath Day Holy	Be of Good Cheer
Repentance	Sacrament Prayers	Great Shall Be Your Joy
Pray Always	Spirit of Revelation	Search the Scriptures

D & C 64:9–11	Word of Wisdom	Forgive One Another
D & C 58:42–43	D & C 8:2–3	D & C 89
D & C 18:10, 15–16	D & C 59:9–10	D & C 20:77, 79

**D & C
61:36**

**D & C
1:37–38**

**D & C
10:5**

6

Listening to the Holy Ghost
D & C 8:2–3

Advance Preparation

1. Find a stick for the Happy Face activity (a ruler or yardstick works well).
2. Scriptures and marking pencils.
3. May ask family members to prepare to tell about a time when the Holy Ghost helped them in some way.
4. A small object for the Hot or Cold game.

Activity: Happy Face

The family sits in a circle. The leader, who knows how to play the game, uses a stick to draw a circle on the floor and then says, "Here is a happy face." The leader then draws two eyes, a nose, and a mouth, while saying, "Here is an eye; here is another eye; here is the nose; and here is the mouth." The leader then clears his or her throat and asks for a volunteer to do *exactly* what the leader has done.

The leader gives the stick to the volunteer, who then tries to duplicate the leader's actions. The secret of the game is that the artist clears his or her throat when the drawing is finished. This can be done somewhat sneakily so that it is not too apparent. This means that the next person has to clear his or her throat also upon finishing in order to do exactly what the leader did.

The leader may have to do it several times and several people may take a turn before someone finally catches on to the secret and does it correctly. Play continues until everyone catches on or gives up.

Scripture

This game teaches us that we need to listen as well as look as we go through this life. If we listen very carefully, we can receive guidance and direction from the Holy Ghost. Doctrine and Covenants 8:2–3 tells us two ways we receive promptings from the Holy Ghost. (The Holy Ghost speaks to our hearts, and to our minds.)

Have the family members read and mark the scripture together and ask them what the two ways are that the Holy Ghost speaks to us. Having the Holy Ghost speak to our hearts might mean that we receive feelings such as love, peace, assurance, confidence, and warmth. Having the Holy Ghost speak to our minds might mean receiving thoughts and ideas.

Sharing

Have family members share experiences of receiving help from the Holy Ghost. Here are two simple stories that can be used if desired.

Story One: One winter during the late 1800s there was a heavy snowstorm in the mountains surrounding Pinedale, Arizona. Two days after the storm, a man named Robert Tyler was under a sawmill shed, figuring up a lumber bill. He had only been under the shed a short period of time when he received a strong feeling that he should move because the shed was going to fall.

Robert walked about fifteen feet away from the shed and, in just a few moments, the entire shed gave way and the heavy roof, loaded with snow, crashed to the ground. If Robert had not responded to the whisperings of the Holy Ghost, he would have been crushed to death. (See Robert M. Tyler, *Faith Promoting Incidents in the Life of Robert M. Tyler* [N.p., 1926], pp. 9–10.)

Story Two: In the year 1920 John Q. Adams and his family were serving in the Samoan Mission. Their eight-year-old daughter was having a birthday party and all were having a great time, when Brother Adams received the impression that he should leave the party and cross the river, which was not far away. Because he could see no reason why he should do this, he ignored the feeling. The impression came a second time, even stronger than before, but once again he decided not to do so. The same feeling came a third time, but this time he saw a certain spot where he should go.

When the feeling would not leave him, he crossed the river bridge and began climbing the slope on the other side. He hadn't gone far before someone called out to him. He soon found one of the Church members who was in serious need of his assistance. This man had accidentally cut an artery in his foot while cutting kindling wood and was bleeding badly.

The injured man could not walk, and Brother Adams could not carry him, so he ran quickly for help. The man fainted before they were able to get him home. However, through prayer, faith, and good care, the man recovered.

Because Brother Adams finally heeded the promptings of the Holy Ghost, the man's life was saved and he became one of the area's best missionaries. (See Jeremiah Stokes, *Modern Miracles* [Salt Lake City: Bookcraft, 1945], pp. 56–58.)

Game: Hot or Cold

Everyone leaves the room except for one person, who hides a small object such as a coin, key, or thimble. Most of the object needs to be in plain sight. The rest of the family then returns to the room and searches for the object. When someone spots the object, he or she sits down and yells out some prearranged comment such as "Hot dog," or "I know where it is." The rest of the family continues to hunt until everyone has found the object.

If the object is difficult to find, the players can ask for help. The person who hid the object then tells the players, based on how close they are to the object, whether they are hot or cold. The closer they are to the object, the hotter they are. The one helping can use words such as "You are in the deep freeze," or "You are getting warmer," or "You are burning up."

When everyone has found the hidden object, the person who found it first gets to hide it, and the game continues.

Application of Hot or Cold

Sometimes we can solve problems by ourselves, but many times we need to listen for the direction of the Holy Ghost.

7

Listen Carefully

Advance Preparation

1. Pen or pencil for each family member.
2. Cut out the topic title strips found at the end of this lesson.
3. Cut out the picture title strips found at the end of this lesson.
4. Review Scripture March rules found in the chapter "Key Scripture Ideas" and choose the Key Scripture cards to be used with the game.

Activity

1. Put the topic title strips in a bowl.
2. Begin by having someone draw one of the strips out of the bowl and start talking about the topic written on the paper. (Someone older should go first so the younger members of the family can see how it is to be done.) As the person talks about the topic, he or she is to slip in things that are not true. The other family members should listen carefully and yell "stop" when they think something has been said that is wrong. They must say what it is that is wrong. This activity could end after each person has had a turn talking about a topic or when all of the strips have been drawn.

Explain to the family that this activity is much like the way Satan works. He mixes truth with lies. Just as we had to listen carefully to the things each person was telling us, we must also listen carefully to what we are told in the world. There are many things that may sound good but that are really Satan's traps. Sometimes the only way we can recognize these lies is to listen carefully to the things that Heavenly Father teaches us.

Have the family name all the ways they can think of that we can listen to Heavenly Father's voice. (Answers might include prayer, thinking, reading scriptures, asking someone you trust.) This would be a good time to review some of the things taught in lesson 2.

Activity

1. Put the picture title strips in a bowl.
2. Give each family member a pen or pencil and a piece of paper.
3. Have each person draw out of the bowl one strip and draw a picture to fit the title. They should include several wrong things in the picture.
4. When everyone is done, each person, one at a time, shows his or her picture to the rest of the family. The other family members write down everything they can see that is wrong in the picture. They score a point for each thing they identify correctly.

This activity is a good example of how Satan not only mixes lies with truth but also tries to make something wrong look right. Have the family name some ways that Satan tries to make evil look good. (You may want to discuss TV ads, music used in wrong ways, so-called "fun" activities which can really be harmful, and so on.)

Key Scripture Review

Review the ten key scriptures marked in lesson 5 by playing Scripture March (the rules are found in the chapter "Key Scripture Ideas"). Family members may use their bookmarks if desired, but they should start trying to do these activities without them. Younger children may need to use them longer than the older members of the family.

Topic Titles

How to make cookies

How to wash a dog

How to clean your bedroom

How to wash your hair

How to make and eat an ice-cream cone

How to watch TV and eat at the same time

How to brush your teeth from start to finish

How to get dressed in the morning

How to make a sandwich

How to clean the bathroom

How to set the table

Describe a sacrament meeting

Picture Titles

A man walking his dog

Joseph Smith in the Sacred Grove

A schoolroom

A kitchen

A zoo

A farm

A family

A car, a truck, and a bus

Two missionaries

Your bishop

A garden

A church

8

The Coming Forth of the Book of Mormon

Advance Preparation

1. Cut out the four secret message squares located at the end of this lesson.
2. Individual copies of the Book of Mormon and marking pencils.
3. Pencils and paper for the Match Game.

Activity: Secret Message

Divide the family into two, three, or four groups. Give each group a copy of the secret message and ask them to decode it. (The message is "If you read the Book of Mormon and pray about it, the Holy Ghost will tell you it is true.")

Story: The Coming Forth of the Book of Mormon

For three years after his first vision, Joseph worked on his father's farm and tried to prepare himself to serve the Lord. One night, in his bedroom, Joseph prayed very hard that he would be forgiven of his sins and would know what the Lord wanted him to do.

Suddenly a light appeared in Joseph's bedroom and an angel appeared at his bedside. The angel said that his name was Moroni and that God had a great work for Joseph to do. Moroni told Joseph about a book written on plates of gold. This book told about a people who had lived in America many hundreds of years before.

The angel also said that there were two stones buried with the plates and that these stones would help Joseph translate the language on the plates into English. These stones were called the Urim and Thummim. Moroni said that Joseph would not receive the plates right away, and Joseph was shown in vision the hill where the plates were buried. Moroni also told Joseph that when he received the plates, he was not to show them to anyone else unless God told him to.

Moroni appeared to Joseph two more times during the night and told him many other things. He was told not to use the gold plates to get rich. The three visits of Moroni lasted all night.

The next morning, Joseph tried to work in the fields with his father but he was too weak because of his experiences during the night. His father told him to go back home, but as Joseph was headed there, the angel Moroni appeared to him again. Moroni told him to tell his father about the plates. When Joseph did as he was instructed, his father believed him and said, "It is of God. Go and do the things that the angel has told you to do."

Because of the vision from the previous night, Joseph recognized the place in the Hill Cumorah where the plates were buried. Seeing the large round stone that covered the plates, Joseph found a lever and used it to raise the stone. Inside were the gold plates and the Urim and Thummim, just as Moroni had told him. Moroni then appeared to him and taught him about the power of Satan, so that Joseph would be strengthened to resist Satan's influence and to keep the commandments. Joseph was commanded to return to the Hill Cumorah at the same time every year for the next four years to receive more teachings from Moroni.

At the end of the four years, Joseph was given the plates of gold. Many people tried to get the plates so they could sell them for money. So Joseph had to keep hiding them and couldn't work much on translating them. He finally moved with his wife to Pennsylvania so he could begin translating the plates.

Because Joseph had to work alone on the translation, and because he had to spend time providing for his family, the translation of the plates went very slowly. He prayed that God would send someone to help him, and God answered him by sending a schoolteacher named Oliver Cowdery.

Because of persecution, Oliver and Joseph had to leave Pennsylvania. They moved to Fayette, New York, where the Whitmer family gave them a place to work. Soon the translation was completed and the book was ready to be taken to the printer.

Special precautions were made to make sure the finished copy of the Book of Mormon was not lost or stolen. Oliver Cowdery made a second copy of the manuscript and a few pages of the copy were taken to the printer as needed. A guard always went with Oliver to and from the printing office. The original copy was kept at the Smiths' home and another guard watched over it.

Soon five thousand copies of the Book of Mormon had been printed, and people began to read the great words written by prophets hundreds of years before.

Joseph Smith said that we can get closer to God by following the teachings found in the Book of Mormon than by following the teachings of any other book. We need to take advantage of the opportunity we have and read the Book of Mormon every day.

Scripture

Have each member of the family turn to Moroni 10:3–5 and read and mark the verses together. Now would be a good time to start a Book of Mormon reading program if you don't already have one as a family.

The Match Game

How well do the members of your family know each other? They will now have an opportunity to find out.

1. Give each family member a pencil and a piece of paper. Younger children can be paired with older family members, or they can just state rather than write down their answers.

2. Read all fifteen questions and ask family members to write their own answers.

3. Read question number 1 again and have each person write down what he or she thinks most of the family members answered. Then have each person read his or her personal answer. One point is received for each match with another family member. Question 2 is then read, answered, matched, and so on.

1. What is your favorite holiday other than Christmas?
2. What is your favorite flavor of ice cream?
3. What is your favorite television show?
4. Who is you favorite person in the Book of Mormon?
5. What food that is not a dessert do you like the best?
6. What is your favorite sport?
7. What is your favorite color?
8. What is your favorite animal at the zoo?
9. Name a person you admire a great deal in the ward or branch?
10. What is an important quality a friend should have?

11. What is an important thing to do to gain a testimony?
12. Name one of the latter-day prophets other than Joseph Smith.
13. Name one of the living Apostles.
14. Name one of the Primary songs.
15. What do you like to do most with the family?

(If you want to continue playing, take turns coming up with other things that you can match.)

Secret Message

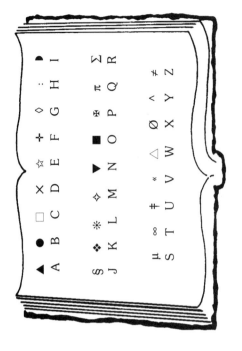

Secret Message

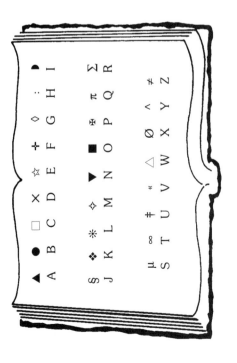

Secret Message

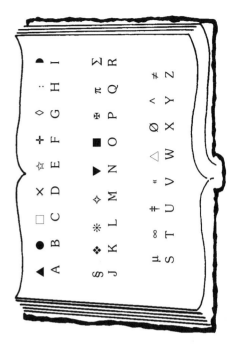

Secret Message

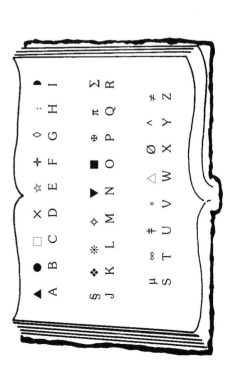

9

Read My Mind

Advance Preparation

1. Review Beat the Leader rules in the chapter "Key Scripture Ideas" and choose the Key Scripture cards to be used with the game.

Activity

1. Begin by having one family member think of an object, event, person, or something else.

2. Each family member takes a turn trying to read the mind of the person by asking a yes-or-no question. Continue until someone guesses what the person is thinking about.

3. Play more rounds until everyone has had a turn at having his or her mind read.

4. Next, ask the person who began the first-round questioning to think of something new. It can be anything that pops into mind.

5. The other family members then take turns reading the mind of the person by telling what they think the person is thinking about. This time they cannot ask questions; they just make up something. They also have to tell how they decided what the person was thinking. (Again, they just make up something fun; for example, they might say, "I could tell what you're thinking by the smile on your face" or "I could tell what you're thinking by the way your hair is combed.")

6. After everyone has had a turn at guessing, the person tells what he or she was really thinking.

7. Play continues until everyone has had a turn at having his or her mind read.

Application

Ask the family to name the only person who can really read our minds. (Heavenly Father.) Explain that we will be judged not only by the things we do but also by the things we think. Our thoughts determine our actions. Discuss with the family how important it is to control our thoughts.

Words from an Apostle

Read the following by Elder Boyd K. Packer:

"Somewhere near your home there is a vacant corner lot. Although adjoining yards may be well tended, a vacant corner lot somehow is always full of weeds.

"There is a footpath across it, a bicycle trail, and ordinarily it is a collecting place for junk. First someone threw a few lawn clippings there. They would not hurt anything. Someone added a few sticks and limbs from a nearby yard. Then came a few papers and a plastic bag, and finally some tin cans and old bottles were included.

"And there it was—a junkyard.

"The neighbors did not intend it to be that. But little contributions from here and there made it so.

"This corner lot is like, so very much like, the minds of many of us. We leave our minds vacant and empty and open to trespass by anyone. Whatever is dumped there we keep.

"We would not consciously permit anyone to dump junk into our minds, not old cans and bottles. But after lawn clippings and papers, the other things just don't seem all that much worse.

"Our minds can become veritable junk heaps with dirty cast-off ideas that accumulate there little by little.

"Years ago I put up some signs in my mind. They are very clearly printed and simply read: No Trespassing, No Dumping Allowed. On occasions it has been necessary to show them very plainly to others.

"I do not want anything coming into my mind that does not have some useful purpose or some value that makes it worth keeping. I have enough trouble keeping the weeds down that sprout there on their own without permitting someone else to clutter my mind with things that do not edify . . . .

"I've had to evict some thoughts a hundred times before they would stay out. I have never been successful until I have put something edifying in their place." (*"That All May Be Edified"* [Salt Lake City: Bookcraft, 1982], pp. 64–65.)

Application

Suggest to the family that a verse of scripture or a song could be used to evict bad thoughts. Have everyone pick a scripture or song that can be used to help keep thoughts clean. Have each family member share with the rest of the family the scripture or song he or she has chosen.

Key Scripture Review

Review the ten key scriptures by playing Beat the Leader. The rules are found in the chapter "Key Scripture Ideas."

10

Pray Always
D & C 10:5

Advance Preparation

1. Cut out the word strips found at the end of the lesson. Keep each full set together! (Notice that the words that go together have the same background design; this should help you separate them if the different sets become accidentally mixed.) Put each full set in a separate envelope. (You'll need four envelopes for the four sets.)
2. Scriptures and marking pencils for each family member.

Activity: Unscramble a Scripture

Divide the family into four groups (small families could use fewer groups). Give each group an envelope containing the word strips that have been cut out. Tell them that when the words are placed in correct order, they will spell out the first part of a Doctrine and Covenants scripture. Explain that the first group to place the words in correct order will be the winners. They cannot remove the word strips from the envelopes until you say go. The words should finally read, "Pray always, that you may come off conqueror; yea, that you may conquer Satan."

Scripture

Ask everyone to turn to and read all of Doctrine and Covenants 10:5. Have the family mark and discuss the scripture together.

You may desire to include one or both of the following ideas in your discussion:

1. Describe a time when prayer has helped you conquer Satan or one of his servants. Other members of the family could also share experiences they have had.

2. To pray always would include having a prayer in our hearts. You might describe a time when you felt the need for help so much that you carried a prayer in your heart throughout the day. If we feel the need for God's constant help in our lives, we can always have a prayer in our hearts. It means that we can pray anytime and anywhere.

Activity

Use some of the following activities or ideas and/or some of your own to help the family memorize part or all of Doctrine and Covenants 10:5.

1. Memorize a few words at a time and have each family member repeat them. Follow this up by pointing at family members and having them give a word or group of words in the right order.

2. After working on the scripture for a few minutes, divide the family into two groups. Give the first word of the scripture. Then have each person in group one, in order, say the word that comes next until someone misses a word. Then say the first word to group two

and let them do the same thing. The group that can get the most words in a row before missing is considered the winner. You may want to do this several times.

3. Time individual family members to see who can say the scripture, without making an error, in the least amount of time. The record may be posted and during each family home evening someone could challenge the record. This would keep the family studying the scripture.

4. Have two teams line up so that two people (one from each team) are competing with each other. Start reading or giving the scripture. When you stop, the first person to give the next word goes to the end of his team's line. The person who didn't give the answer must move out of his team's line and does not compete for the rest of the round. Two new people are now at the front of the lines. The reader continues reciting the scripture. When he stops, the two new front people try to give the next word. When one team has no players standing, the other team is declared the winner.

5. Now have the teams scramble the word strips again and see who can most quickly put the scripture in order. Time the teams and establish a record to beat.

6. Have a relay game. Place the word strips in scrambled sets on one side of the room. Two or more teams line up on the other side of the room. Team members have to take turns running to the word strips and bringing one strip back until all of the strips have been retrieved and placed in their proper order. The teams can compete with each other or you can set a certain time limit and see if all of the teams can beat it. You can do this several times, lowering the time limit each time.

Just relax and have a good time, and by the end of any of these activities most of the family members will remember the scripture very well.

always	Pray
you	that
come	may
conqueror;	off
that	yea,
may	you
Satan	conquer

always	Pray
you	that
come	may
conqueror;	off
that	yea,
may	you
Satan	conquer

Pray	always
that	you
may	come
off	conqueror;
yea,	that
you	may
conquer	Satan

Pray	always
that	you
may	come
off	conqueror;
yea,	that
you	may
conquer	Satan

11

Family Draw

Advance Preparation

1. Label three bowls "Objects," "Places," and "Miscellaneous."
2. Cut out all of the category strips found at the end of this lesson, and place the strips in their respective category bowls.

Activity

1. One of the family members begins by choosing a category and then drawing a strip out of the corresponding category bowl. Using a piece of paper or a chalkboard that the other family members can see, the person draws picture clues to match the item given on the strip of paper. As the person draws, the rest of the family tries to guess what the strip of paper says. The picture cannot have any words or letters in it.

2. The first person to guess the correct answer scores five points and an additional five points if he can tell what the picture has to do with the gospel. He then gets to choose the next category, select a strip of paper, and draw picture clues.

3. If a person who has already had a turn to draw guesses what the picture is, he gets ten points and chooses someone who hasn't had a turn to draw.

4. Play continues until all of the bowls are empty.

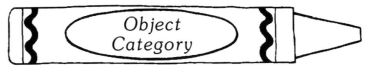

Object Category

Sacrament Tray

Gold Plates

Liahona

Bishop's Office

Altar

Fig Tree

John Taylor's Pocket Watch

Hymnbook

Seed

Joseph's Coat of Many Colors

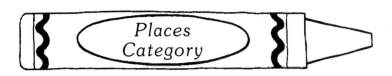

Places
Category

Salt Lake City

Jerusalem

Dead Sea

Kirtland, Ohio

Sea of Galilee

Celestial Kingdom

Garden of Eden

Jordan River

Bethlehem

Hill Cumorah

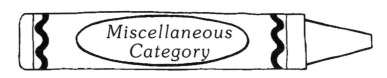
Miscellaneous Category

Aaronic Priesthood

Repentance

Faith

Apostle

Angels

Prophet

Elder

Moses

Fasting

Shepherd

12

Restoration of the Priesthood

Advance Preparation

1. Cut out letter squares found at end of lesson. Scramble the letters and place them in two envelopes. The shaded letters go in one envelope, and the unshaded letters go in the other envelope.
2. Marking pencils and scriptures for each family member.
3. Cut out the answer slips at the end of the lesson. Place the four sets in separate envelopes labeled, "Numbered Chairs Game—Set 1," "Numbered Chairs Game—Set 2," etc.
4. Review the Numbered Chairs game in "Games for Many Occasions."

Activity: Scrambled Letters

Divide the family into two teams and give each team one of the envelopes containing the scrambled letters. Give them these instructions:

1. Your job is to make words out of these scrambled letters.
2. Each envelope contains nine words that have something to do with the priesthood.
3. Take out one square and look at it. In the bottom left corner is a number. All the letters in this word are marked with the same number. For each word, all the numbers will match.
4. All team members may work together on the same word or you may organize so that different people are working on each word. On the word *go*, dump the letters out and start working. The team that correctly spells all nine words first wins the game (but doesn't rub it in since they are "celestial people").

When both teams have spelled all of the words *(Melchizedek, Aaronic, Baptism, Apostle, Deacon, Healings, Power, Magnify,* and *Confirm),* move to the next part of the lesson.

Pretest

To see how much the family knows about the restoration of the priesthood, ask them to decide whether the following statements are true or false (the correct answers immediately follow the statements):
  1. The Melchizedek Priesthood was restored by Peter, James, and John. (True.)
  2. The Aaronic Priesthood was restored by the angel Moroni. (False.)
  3. The Church was restored before the priesthood was restored. (False.)
  4. Joseph was alone when he received the Aaronic Priesthood. (False.)
  5. Oliver Cowdery was with Joseph when the Melchizedek Priesthood was restored. (True.)

6. The Aaronic Priesthood has the authority to give the gift of the Holy Ghost. (False.)

7. The Aaronic Priesthood has the authority to baptize. (True.)

8. The Aaronic Priesthood was given to Joseph Smith in the Sacred Grove where he received the First Vision. (False.)

9. The Aaronic Priesthood holds the keys for the gospel of repentance. (True.)

10. Joseph Smith was the first person baptized after the priesthood was restored. (False.)

Story and Scripture

Have family members take turns reading sections of the following story of the restoration of the priesthood. Have them especially listen for the correct answers to the pretest.

Joseph and Oliver learned many things while they were translating the Book of Mormon. One of these things was the importance of baptism. They learned that they must be baptized for the remission of sins, yet neither of them had been baptized. Since they did not have authority to baptize each other, they wondered what they should do.

The Susquehanna River was just a short distance away, and on May 15, 1829, Joseph and Oliver knelt near the river and asked God about baptism. John the Baptist, the same person who baptized Jesus, appeared to them and bestowed upon them the Aaronic Priesthood.

Stop the story at this point and have the family turn to section 13 of the Doctrine and Covenants to find out what John the Baptist said. Mark and discuss with the family the three keys that are held by the Aaronic Priesthood: 1. ministering of angels (to "minister" is to teach and nurture); 2. the gospel of repentance; 3. baptism by immersion for the remission of sins. Talk about how important these three things are and then continue with the story.

John the Baptist was a resurrected person, and he told Joseph and Oliver that he was sent by Peter, James, and John, the three chief Apostles at the time of Jesus. He said that the Aaronic Priesthood did not have the authority to confer the gift of the Holy Ghost, but he promised that Joseph and Oliver would soon receive this authority.

John then commanded Joseph and Oliver to baptize each other. Joseph baptized Oliver, and then Oliver baptized Joseph. They then ordained each other to the Aaronic Priesthood. Joseph's younger brother Samuel was baptized ten days later.

Just a short time later, Peter, James, and John conferred the Melchizedek Priesthood upon Joseph and Oliver. They now had the power to give the gift of the Holy Ghost. These ancient Apostles also gave them the same keys of the priesthood that they had received from Jesus. This gave them the power to organize the true Church of Jesus Christ, which would soon be established on the earth.

Have the family take the pretest again and see if they can get 100 percent of the answers correct.

Numbered Chairs

Use the four envelopes of answer slips and the following questions to play the game Numbered Chairs (see the rules for Numbered Chairs in the chapter "Games for Many Occasions"). After ten of the questions have been used, the points could be totaled up, a winner declared, and a new game started. This would give a fresh start to those teams who are behind. All twenty of the answer slips would still be passed out before the first game begins. (Correct answers appear in parentheses immediately following the questions.)

1. God did not tell us to merely read the scriptures but to do what? (Search.)
2. Who was rebaptized because he was first baptized in a bathtub? (Spencer W. Kimball.)
3. Who was the only Church President born outside the United States? (John Taylor.)
4. How old was Joseph when he received the First Vision? (Fourteen.)
5. What was Joseph told about which church to join? (Join none of them.)
6. What are two ways we receive promptings from the Holy Ghost? (In the heart, and in the mind.)
7. In which hill were the gold plates buried? (Cumorah.)
8. Who became scribe for Joseph and helped him finish translating the Book of Mormon? (Oliver Cowdery.)
9. What book in the Bible did Joseph read that helped him decide to pray? (James.)
10. Who appeared to Joseph in the First Vision? (Heavenly Father and Jesus.)

11. How many years passed between the First Vision and Moroni's appearance to Joseph in his bedroom? (Three.)
12. What were the stones called that were buried with the gold plates? (Urim and Thummim.)
13. Which family gave Joseph a place to stay so he could finish the Book of Mormon? (Whitmer.)
14. After his first visit to the hill, how many more times did Joseph meet the angel at Cumorah? (Four.)
15. Who restored the Aaronic Priesthood? (John the Baptist.)
16. Who restored the Melchizedek Priesthood? (Peter, James, and John.)
17. Which priesthood was restored first? (Aaronic.)
18. What is one of the keys of the Aaronic Priesthood? (Ministering of angels.)
19. Which priesthood has the authority to give the gift of the Holy Ghost? (Melchizedek.)
20. What can a person do to get a testimony of the Book of Mormon? (Read and pray.)

M (1)	E (1)	L (1)	C (1)	H (1)
I (1)	Z (1)	E (1)	D (1)	E (1)
K (1)	A (2)	A (2)	R (2)	O (2)
N (2)	I (2)	C (2)	B (3)	A (3)
P (3)	T (3)	I (3)	S (3)	M (3)
A (4)	P (4)	O (4)	S (4)	T (4)
L (4)	E (4)	D (5)	E (5)	A (5)
C (5)	O (5)	N (5)	H (6)	E (6)
A (6)	L (6)	I (6)	N (6)	G (6)
S (6)	P (7)	O (7)	W (7)	E (7)
R (7)	M (8)	A (8)	G (8)	N (8)
I (8)	F (8)	Y (8)	C (9)	O (9)
N (9)	F (9)	I (9)	R (9)	M (9)

M (1)	E (1)	L (1)	C (1)	H (1)
I (1)	Z (1)	E (1)	D (1)	E (1)
K (1)	A (2)	A (2)	R (2)	O (2)
N (2)	I (2)	C (2)	B (3)	A (3)
P (3)	T (3)	I (3)	S (3)	M (3)
A (4)	P (4)	O (4)	S (4)	T (4)
L (4)	E (4)	D (5)	E (5)	A (5)
C (5)	O (5)	N (5)	H (6)	E (6)
A (6)	L (6)	I (6)	N (6)	G (6)
S (6)	P (7)	O (7)	W (7)	E (7)
R (7)	M (8)	A (8)	G (8)	N (8)
I (8)	F (8)	Y (8)	C (9)	O (9)
N (9)	F (9)	I (9)	R (9)	M (9)

Set 1	Search	Melchizedek
John Taylor	Fourteen	Spencer W. Kimball
In the heart and mind	Cumorah	Join none of them
James	Heavenly Father and Jesus	Oliver Cowdery
Urim and Thummim	God and Jesus	Three
John the Baptist	Whitmer	Four
Ministering of angels	Peter, James, and John	Aaronic

Set 2	Search	Spencer W. Kimball
John Taylor	Fourteen	Join none of them
In the heart and mind	Cumorah	Oliver Cowdery
James	Heavenly Father and Jesus	Three
Urim and Thummim	Whitmer	Four
John the Baptist	Peter, James, and John	Aaronic
Ministering of angels	Melchizedek	Read and pray

Set 3	Search	Spencer W. Kimball
John Taylor	Fourteen	Join none of them
In the heart and mind	Cumorah	Oliver Cowdery
James	Heavenly Father and Jesus	Three
Urim and Thummim	Whitmer	Four
John the Baptist	Peter, James, and John	Aaronic
Ministering of angels	Melchizedek	Read and pray

Set 4	Search	Spencer W. Kimball
John Taylor	Fourteen	Join none of them
In the heart and mind	Cumorah	Oliver Cowdery
James	Heavenly Father and Jesus	Three
Urim and Thummim	Whitmer	Four
John the Baptist	Peter, James, and John	Aaronic
Ministering of angels	Melchizedek	Read and pray

13

Useless Without

Advance Preparation

1. A pencil and paper for each person in the family.
2. Review the rules for game All or Nothing found in the chapter ``Key Scripture Ideas'' and prepare the necessary materials.

Activity

1. Divide the family into pairs. Younger children should be paired up with the older ones.

2. Explain to the family that they will have three minutes to make a list of things that are useless without something else. Give them the following examples: A lamp is useless without a light bulb; a pen is useless without ink; a car is useless without gas.

3. When the time is up, have each group share what they have written down. They score one point for each set and a bonus point if no one else has it.

4. Explain to the family that there are many things in the gospel that are useless without other things. Using the statements at the end of the lesson, have each group write down as many things as they can to fill in the blanks. They will have thirty seconds for each statement.

5. After the time is up, each team shares the things they have written down and how the one makes the other useful. They receive a point for each item and a bonus point if no one else has written the answer.

6. Explain to the family that, most important of all, *we* are useless without God and all of the things that he has given us. We should recognize God's hand in our lives and thank him for his help. Conclude by having the family read and mark Doctrine and Covenants 59:20–21.

Suggestion: If you have access to the *Family Home Evening Video Supplement 2* containing "The Touch of the Master's Hand," showing it would be an effective way of concluding your lesson.

Key Scripture Review

Play the game All or Nothing using the ten key scriptures.

A body is useless without _____.

The scriptures are useless without _____.

Death is useless without _____.

A leader is useless without _____.

The priesthood is useless without _____.

Repentance is useless without _____.

The resurrection is useless without _____.

A prophet is useless without _____.

A blessing is useless without _____.

Faith is useless without _____.

A family is useless without _____.

Baptism is useless without _____.

A temple marriage is useless without _____.

You are useless without _____.

14

Worth of a Soul
D & C 18:10–16

Advance Preparation

1. Look at the activity Of Most Worth. The products and prices used in this activity were obtained in 1991 in our local area. You may wish to replace ours with some from your local stores.
2. Review the rules for the game Name That Price found in the chapter "Games for Many Occasions."
3. Cut out the Name That Price game pieces found at the end of this lesson and place them in an envelope labeled "Name That Price."
4. Individual scriptures and marking pencils.
5. A pencil and piece of paper for each family member.

Activity: Of Most Worth

The object of the activity is to see which teams or individuals can tell which items cost the most.

1. Give each individual or team a piece of paper and a pencil.

2. Read the three products that are grouped together and have each individual or team rank them from the most expensive (first) to the least expensive (third). Make sure you read the items below out of order when reading them the first time. *Do not* read the prices yet.

3. Now, read the ranking and price of the items. Teams receive one point for each product they had in the correct ranking.

4. After all three rounds of the activity have been finished, each individual or team adds up their score and the one with the most points is the winner.

Inexpensive training wheels	$6.96
24" Bicycle tire	$4.97
24" Bicycle tube	$2.47
Two cream-filled cupcakes	69 cents
One can of soda pop	38 cents
One Popsicle (double)	16 cents
Monopoly game	$9.97
Wooden dominoes (55 pieces)	$5.36
Chutes and Ladders game	$4.97

Scripture

Tell the family that this lesson has to do with something of greater value than anything a person can purchase, then have them turn to Doctrine and Covenants 18:10–16.

97

Pair younger children with older family members and do the following activities.

1. Have the family respond to the question "What does verse 10 say God wants us to remember?" (The worth of souls is great in his sight.)

2. Have the family tell why they feel we are of great worth to God. (We are his children; he loves us a great deal; we have the capacity to become gods; and so on.)

3. There are three important words that are used three different times in verses 15 and 16. Ask your family to identify these three words and to circle them in their copies of the scriptures each time they are used in verses 15 and 16. (*Soul, great,* and *joy* are each used three times.)

4. Have the family define what these three words mean.

5. The Lord promises that our joy shall be great if we cry repentance and help even one person come unto him. Have each family member explain one thing he or she can do to cry repentance.

6. Tell your family how much you love them and how valuable they are to you. Remind them that God knows them even better than you do and loves them a great deal. Point out to them that they are spiritual brothers and sisters as well as physical ones and that *every* person is precious.

Game: Name That Price

One of the best ways to cry repentance is to serve a full-time mission. All of the products used in this game are things that missionaries may have to buy when preparing for their missions.

Lay the price cards face down where the family will be able to see them when they are uncovered. Place each product square on top of the matching price. You are now ready to play the game.

The instructions for playing the game are found in the chapter "Games for Many Occasions." You can use the following information to explain each product as it is introduced.

Inexpensive long-sleeved white shirt	$11.93
Least expensive tie in national chain of stores	$5.97
Real leather Bible and triple combination with book tabs	$77.00
Medium-priced alarm clock (both wind-up and electric models)	$8.24
Men's pajamas (cotton top and bottom)	$10.93
Medium-priced Walkman cassette player	$49.76
Missionary journal, hardbound, information for mission in front	$6.95
Large hard-shell suitcase, with wheels, three-year warranty	$62.94
Camera, national brand, 35 mm for slides and prints, auto focus, inexpensive but not cheapest	$74.83

$11.93	**$5.97**	**$77.00**
$8.24	**$10.93**	**$49.76**
$6.95	**$62.94**	**$74.83**

15

Small and Simple Things

Advance Preparation

1. Cut out the three-letter word cards and the category cards for the game Three-Letter Panic (these are found at the end of this lesson).
2. Cut out the Presidents of the Church fact cards found at the end of this lesson.
3. Numbered squares envelope.
4. Presidents of the Church envelope.

Game: Three-Letter Panic

1. Divide the family into two teams.
2. Place the three-letter word cards face down on a table or the floor.
3. Place the category cards face down next to the three-letter word cards.
4. Begin play by having one of the teams turn over the first category card. They then turn over the top three-letter word card. They have thirty seconds to give three names of people, places, objects, or teachings that start with each of the three letters of the word. The three words must fit the selected category. For example, if the three-letter word card turned over said *tag* and the category selected was *Book of Mormon,* the team members could say "Tree of life, Alma, and Gadianton."
5. At the end of the thirty seconds, the team receives one point for each acceptable answer.
6. Play alternates between teams until all of the three-letter word cards have been turned over. When all of the category cards have been turned over, shuffle them and continue play.

Application

Have the family read, mark, and discuss Doctrine and Covenants 64:33. Explain to the family that just as the teams made a lot of words out of the three-letter words, so small things can become big things. The Book of Mormon is a good example. It is one small book, but it has changed the lives of millions of people. Have the family name things which are small and simple but which have brought about great things. Then discuss some little things that family members could do to make the family better.

Game: Concentration

1. Using the fact cards, briefly review as a family the facts on the Presidents of the Church. One method is to read the facts and then have family members take turns guessing who the President is.
2. Choose nine of the Presidents of the Church picture cards (used in lesson 3) and the matching nine Presidents of the Church fact cards.

3. Place the nine Presidents of the Church picture cards face down in a row on the floor or table. Place the nine fact cards in another row face down next to the picture cards.

4. Cover the picture cards with numbered squares 1 through 9 and the fact cards with numbered squares 10 through 18.

5. Divide the family into two groups. Have the first group choose a number from each row. They then look at each by picking up both the number card and the picture or fact card and turning them over so that both a picture and a fact list are showing. If the facts match the picture, the first group keeps the cards and the second group takes the next turn. If the first group does *not* find a match, they place the numbers back over the cards and the second group takes the next turn. (Notice that even if a match is made, only one attempt can be made each turn.)

6. Play alternates between teams until all nine of the matches have been made. The group with the most matches wins the game.

Note: When you are finished you should put the Presidents of the Church fact cards with the picture cards in the envelope labeled "Presidents of the Church."

Category Cards

Repentance	**Prophets**	**Tithing**
Bible	**Commandments**	**Prayer**
Book of Mormon	**Faith**	**Word of Wisdom**

elm

won

fly

ego

her

oar

elf

far

tip

fig	**any**	**oil**
let	**ace**	**die**
get	**tag**	**cry**

1. Received the First Vision (1820) 2. Translated the Book of Mormon 3. Directed to organize the Church (April 6, 1830) 4. Martyred with his brother Hyrum (June 27, 1844)	1. Led pioneers to the Salt Lake Valley (1846–47) 2. Sustained as second President of the Church at Winter Quarters (1847) 3. Known as the "Lion of the Lord" 4. Led the Church longer than any other President (33 yrs.)	1. In jail with Joseph and Hyrum when they were martyred 2. Sustained as third President of the Church (1880) 3. Only Church President born outside the U.S. (England) 4. Known as the "Defender of the Faith"
1. Known for his many accidents as a youth 2. Baptized three hundred people in three months while in England 3. Sustained as fourth President of the Church (1889) 4. Issued the Manifesto which discontinued plural marriage (1890)	1. Helped organize the Perpetual Emigration Fund (1849) 2. First president of the Salt Lake Temple (1893) 3. Sustained as fifth President of the Church (1898) 4. Emphasized the importance of tithing	1. Son of Hyrum and Mary Fielding Smith 2. Sustained as sixth President of the Church (1901) 3. Started the family "Home Evening" program (1915) 4. Received a vision of the spirit world (see D & C 138)
1. Known for his great persistence 2. Sustained as seventh President of the Church (1918) 3. Introduced the Church welfare program (1936) 4. Served second longest as President of the Church (27 yrs.)	1. Known for his great compassion 2. Served on the national executive board of the Boy Scouts of America 3. Sustained as eighth President of the Church (1945) 4. Organized help for the Saints in Europe after World War II	1. Served as principal of Weber Stake Academy 2. Sustained as ninth President of the Church (1951) 3. Apostle longer than any other modern-day Apostle (63 yrs., 9 mos.) 4. The Church expanded worldwide under his leadership

1. Son of Joseph F. Smith and grandson of Hyrum Smith

2. Served as Church historian longer than any other person

3. Known for his great understanding of the scriptures

4. Sustained as tenth President of the Church (1970)

1. Principal of a school at age eighteen

2. Played four musical instruments

3. Sustained as eleventh President of the Church (1972)

4. Served as President of the Church for eighteen months

1. Grandson of Heber C. Kimball

2. Known for his work among the Lamanites

3. Sustained as twelfth President of the Church (1973)

4. Set whirlwind pace of work and travel in spite of physical afflictions

1. Was the oldest of eleven children; all eleven served full-time missions

2. Distributed supplies and visited members in Europe following World War II

3. Served as U.S. Secretary of Agriculture

4. Sustained as thirteenth President of the Church (1985)

16

The Church Is Organized

Advance Preparation

1. Coins and five containers (cups, glasses, jars, or pans) for Coin Toss activity. Label the containers "Faith," "Repentance," "Baptism," "Gift of the Holy Ghost," and "Celestial Kingdom."
2. Paper and pencils.
3. Review rules for the Shell Game found in the chapter "Games for Many Occasions." Collect the required items.
4. Become acquainted with the questions and suggestions found in the chapters "Game Questions" and "Children's Questions."

Activity: Coin Toss

1. Let everyone practice throwing a coin into the containers. (This will also give you a chance to make sure the containers work and to establish how far away family members will need to stand to provide enough challenge.)

2. Place a piece of tape on the floor where family members will have to stand. You may desire to make some closer tape lines for younger family members.

3. Place the containers in a row, the "Faith" container being the closest to the line and the one for the celestial kingdom the farthest away.

4. Have family members take turns trying to throw a coin into the containers. Each person has to successfully throw a coin into the "Faith" container before he or she can try the next container. Only one turn is taken at a time, and the first person to progress to the celestial kingdom is the winner.

5. When everyone has reached the celestial kingdom, have family members return to their seats and then ask them what gospel principle this activity teaches. (Family members progress toward the celestial kingdom by following the first principles and ordinances of the gospel.)

6. Ask the family what great event took place that brought to light these principles and ordinances and made going to the celestial kingdom possible. (The restoration of the Church; the restoration of the priesthood was also necessary and is discussed in lesson 12.)

Activity: How Much Do You Know about the Restoration of the Church?

1. Divide the family into groups.

2. Explain to the family that in our meetings we pray, sing hymns, speak, partake of the sacrament, and so on. During the meeting that was held to organize the Church, at least ten important activities took place.

3. Have each group write down ten activities they think would have taken place during or immediately after this very important meeting.

4. Read the following account of the organization of the Church. Stop after each

activity is mentioned and see whether or not the groups have listed this particular activity. (Each of the ten activities is noted in parentheses.)

Organization of the Church

For ten years after the First Vision, the Lord prepared the way for his true Church to be organized. Joseph was taught, the priesthood was restored, the Book of Mormon was published, and the hearts of many people were touched.

Finally on Tuesday April 6, 1830, the Church was organized. This date was chosen by the Lord. The meeting was held in the Peter Whitmer, Sr., home and was begun with a prayer. *(1. Prayer.)*

New York state law required all religious organizations to be incorporated with three to nine trustees. Fulfilling this requirement, six brethren acted as organizers. Many other people who had accepted the gospel were also present at the meeting.

Joseph Smith asked those present whether or not they were willing to organize the Church and accept himself and Oliver Cowdery as their leaders. Those present unanimously consented. *(2. Sustaining vote by raising of hands.)*

Joseph then laid his hands on the head of Oliver Cowdery and ordained him an elder of the Church of Jesus Christ. Oliver then ordained Joseph to the same office. *(3. Ordained elders.)*

Joseph and Oliver then prepared, administered, and passed the sacrament for the first time in the latter-day Church. *(4. Sacrament.)*

All six of the men who acted as the organizers had been baptized previously for the remission of sins, but they were baptized again on this day as members of the Church of Jesus Christ. *(5. Rebaptisms.)*

All those who had been baptized previously were confirmed members of the Church and given the gift of the Holy Ghost. *(6. Confirmations.)*

During the meeting a revelation was received by Joseph Smith. It was recorded and is known as section 21 in the Doctrine and Covenants. *(7. Revelation received.)*

The Spirit directed Joseph to call and ordain some of the men to different offices in the priesthood. *(8. Priesthood ordinations.)*

Many bore their testimonies and thanked God for the great blessings of the restored Church and gospel. The meeting was then closed. *(9. Bearing of testimonies.)*

Many of those present desired to be baptized, and so soon after they were baptized into the newly restored Church. To the great joy of Joseph Smith, his parents were baptized at that time. *(10. New converts baptized.)*

Even though the Church began with just these few members, millions of people belong to the Church today. It will continue to grow and prepare the earth for the second coming of the Lord.

In 1838 the Lord revealed that the full name of the restored Church should be The Church of Jesus Christ of Latter-day Saints (see D&C 115:4). A *Saint* is a person who is humble, prayerful, and faithful, and who is striving to become like Jesus.

Game: The Shell Game

Play the Shell Game (see the game rules in the chapter "Games For Many Occasions"), using the questions from lessons 1 through 16 found in the "Game Questions" chapter. Children can respond to the questions found in the chapter "Children's Questions."

17

Family Olympics

Advance Preparation

1. Paper and pen or pencil for each team.
2. Masking tape.
3. Cut out events sheets found at the end of this lesson.
4. Make an imitation barbell weight, using a stick (for example, a yardstick) with some fake weights attached to the ends. You may want to tape on balloons.
5. Set of children's blocks (different shapes if possible).
6. Get twenty-five paper cups and write a numeral on the bottom of each, from 1 through 25.
7. Find a golf putter or substitute (a yardstick, for example) and a golf ball or substitute.

Activity: Family Olympics

Divide the family into two or three teams. Choose one person on each team to keep track of his or her team's score.

Event 1: Weight Lifting

Using the imitation barbell, have each member of the family lift the weight, pretending it is very heavy. For example, they could grunt, make an ugly face, etc. Have the rest of the family judge the lift, rating it from one (poor) to ten (excellent). The lift should be judged on how real it looks. Everyone tells the score he or she gave the person, and the person's final rating can be determined by averaging the scores or by adding them all together. Then the next person lifts and receives a rating. At the end of the event, each team receives points equal to the highest rating given to one of the team members.

Event 2: President Find

Give one Event 2 sheet to each team. Read the directions aloud. Allow the teams ten minutes to work on the sheet. At the end of ten minutes, each team receives one point for each name they found in the puzzle.

Event 3: Block It

1. Using a piece of masking tape, make a line at one end of the room. This will be the starting line for the players.
2. Put the blocks in a box at the other end of the room, next to a hard, flat surface (a hardbound book, a little table, etc.).
3. Ask someone to be the timer. He will give the "go" signal and, after exactly one minute, he will call "stop."

117

4. Have one team line up single file behind the line. On the word *go,* the first person in the line runs to the box of blocks, picks up one block, and places the block on the hard surface. Once he has picked up a block, he cannot put it back in the box. He then runs back to the line and the next team member does the same thing. This continues until one minute is up or the blocks tip over.

5. The team scores one point for each block the team stacked if the stack did not fall. There is no score if any blocks fell.

6. The play then rotates to the next team. The game continues until all of the teams have had the opportunity to stack the blocks for one minute.

Event 4: Secret Message

Give each team a sheet for Event 4. Read the directions aloud. Each team that finishes the sheet correctly receives five points. The first team to do it correctly receives a bonus of two points.

Event 5: Cup Shoot

1. Using masking tape, make a line at one end of the room, long enough to place the twenty-five cups on the line. At the other end of the room make another line with masking tape. This will be the putting line.

2. Place the twenty-five numbered cups right side up on the first line, in random order, so the numbers on the bottom can't be seen.

3. Choose someone to be the timer. The time limit is forty-five seconds.

4. One of the team members is chosen as the retriever. This person stands behind the cup line and retrieves the ball for his or her team. The retriever must return the ball to the team by slowly rolling it to them. If the retriever throws the ball in the air, the team is disqualified from the event.

5. Have the rest of the team line up in single file behind the putting line. Place the ball on the line. The object of this event is to knock down the cups with the ball. On the word *go,* the first person putts the ball at the cups, then gives the putter to the next person while the retriever rolls back the ball. The next person putts, and so on. Each person on the team must putt before a person can putt again.

6. At the end of the forty-five seconds, the timer calls "stop." Pick up all the cups that have been knocked off the line and add up the numbers on the bottom for the team's score.

7. Reset the cups on the line in random order and begin play with the next team. Continue until all teams have had a turn.

Conclusion

Some of these events help reinforce ideas and information from your study of Church history and the Doctrine and Covenants. But the other purpose for having them is to encourage family cooperation and consideration. Make them fun and make sure that you're building positive skills and feelings.

Event 2

The FIRST and LAST names of the thirteen Presidents of the Church are in the puzzle below. See if you can find and circle all twenty-six names; they may appear going up, down, diagonally, forward, or backward.

```
Q G J A K J O S E P H Z D D A V I D W G
Q J O S E P H S P E N C E R S N O W R D
S W H M V N P U D E Z B H Y T H E Z R A
U Z V E H O M B E N S O N L P M F I U P
B X H B B N Q J H F B X T E O M M Z N G
Q G A C V E T U L A B N S A N W P I R C
P U K I U N R P V Q R O L O R E N Z O F
V S E D A S M I T H J O A P F K W P M S
K G A R J S D R Y I F B L R G J A A M A
A V G L H F M A D F W R T D P O H I I W
I P G N P V K I U T W Z K W Z G G J N G
F H L Y P C R R T K H I W W I G U E C G
B L Q X M H D J S H I G L R T P E Y U H
K D A V T O B R A D N M B F P L G R Y R
M B Y I O W B L C U Z X B V O Q V P H X
F F M W F C Q R O O E S X A E R Y C A A
C S S T J S Q Y Y X Q Z W S L R D Q X K
W A J W V T Q P M T A Y L O R L N E J G
J F K B M H O Q J O H N N G G E O R G E
N A T Q J X A I M P G Q G U G O U U D I
```

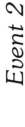
Joseph Smith

Brigham Young

John Taylor

Lorenzo Snow

Joseph Fielding Smith

Wilford Woodruff

David O. McKay

George Albert Smith

Heber J. Grant

Joseph F. Smith

Harold B. Lee

Spencer W. Kimball

Ezra Taft Benson

Event 2

The FIRST and LAST names of the thirteen Presidents of the Church are in the puzzle below. See if you can find and circle all twenty-six names; they may appear going up, down, diagonally, forward, or backward.

```
Q G J A K J O S E P H Z D D A V I D W G
Q J O S E P H S P E N C E R S N O W R D
S W H M V N P U D E Z B H Y T H E Z R A
U Z V E H O M B E N S O N L P M F I U P
B X H B B N Q J H F B X T E O M M Z N G
Q G A C V E T U L A B N S A N W P I R C
P U K I U N R P V Q R O L O R E N Z O F
V S E D A S M I T H J O A P F K W P M S
K G A R J S D R Y I F B L R G J A A M A
A V G L H F M A D F W R T D P O H I I W
I P G N P V K I U T W Z K W Z G G J N G
F H L Y P C R R T K H I W W I G U E C G
B L Q X M H D J S H I G L R T P E Y U H
K D A V T O B R A D N M B F P L G R Y R
M B Y I O W B L C U Z X B V O Q V P H X
F F M W F C Q R O O E S X A E R Y C A A
C S S T J S Q Y Y X Q Z W S L R D Q X K
W A J W V T Q P M T A Y L O R L N E J G
J F K B M H O Q J O H N N G G E O R G E
N A T Q J X A I M P G Q G U G O U U D I
```

Joseph Smith

Brigham Young

John Taylor

Wilford Woodruff

David O. McKay

Lorenzo Snow

Joseph Fielding Smith

George Albert Smith

Heber J. Grant

Joseph F. Smith

Harold B. Lee

Spencer W. Kimball

Ezra Taft Benson

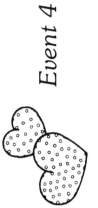

Event 4

Fill in the names of the Presidents of the Church in order. Then using the letters with the numbers you will find out something that all the Presidents of the Church loved.

1. _ _ _ _ 2 _ _ _ _ _ _

2. _ _ _ _ 13 _ _ 14 _ _ _ _

3. _ 1 _ _ _ _ _ _

4. _ _ _ 6 _ _ _ _

5. _ 12 _ _ _ 5 _

6. _ _ _ 3 _ _ _ _

7. _ 4 _ _ _ _

8. _ _ _ _ _ _ _ _ 10

9. _ _ _ 7 _ _ _

10. 11 _ _ _ _ _

11. _ _ _ 8 _ _

12. _ _ _ _ 15 _ _

13. _ 9 _ _ _ _

___ ___ ___ ___ ___ ___ ___
1   2   3   4   5   6   7

___ ___ ___ ___ ___ ___ ___ ___
8   9   10 11 12 13 14 15

Event 2

The FIRST and LAST names of the thirteen Presidents of the Church are in the puzzle below. See if you can find and circle all twenty-six names; they may appear going up, down, diagonally, forward, or backward.

```
Q G J A K J O S E P H Z D D A V I D W G
Q J O S E P H S P E N C E R S N O W R D
S W H M V N P U D E Z B H Y T H E Z R A
U Z V E H O M B E N S O N L P M F I U P
B X H B B N Q J H F B X T E O M M Z N G
Q G A C V E T U L A B N S A N W P I R C
P U K I U N R P V Q R O L O R E N Z O F
V S E D A S M I T H J O A P F K W P M S
K G A R J S D R Y I F B L R G J A A M A
A V G L H F M A D F W R T D P O H I I W
I P G N P V K I U T W Z K W Z G G J N G
F H L Y P C R R T K H I W W I G U E C G
B L Q X M H D J S H I G L R T P E Y U H
K D A V T O B R A D N M B F P L G R Y R
M B Y I O W B L C U Z X B V O Q V P H X
F F M W F C Q R O O E S X A E R Y C A A
C S S T J S Q Y Y X Q Z W S L R D Q X K
W A J W V T Q P M T A Y L O R L N E J G
J F K B M H O Q J O H N N G G E O R G E
N A T Q J X A I M P G G Q G U G O U U D I
```

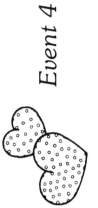

Joseph Smith

Brigham Young

John Taylor

Wilford Woodruff

David O. McKay

Lorenzo Snow

Joseph Fielding Smith

Joseph F. Smith

Harold B. Lee

Heber J. Grant

Spencer W. Kimball

George Albert Smith

Ezra Taft Benson

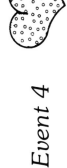
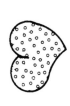

Event 4

Fill in the names of the Presidents of the Church in order. Then using the letters with the numbers you will find out something that all the Presidents of the Church loved.

1. __ __ __ __ __
      2

2. __ __ __ __ __
      13   14

3. __ __ __ __
     1

4. __ __ __ __ __
          6

5. __ __ __ __ __
    12   5

6. __ __ __ __
     3

7. __ __ __
   4

8. __ __ __ __ __
            10

9. __ __ __ __ __
         7

10. __ __ __ __ __
    11

11. __ __ __ __
    8

12. __ __ __ __
    15

13. __ __ __ __ __
          9

__ __ __ __ __ __ __
1   2   3   4   5   6   7

__ __ __ __ __ __ __ __
8   9   10   11   12   13   14   15

Event 4

Fill in the names of the Presidents of the Church in order. Then using the letters with the numbers you will find out something that all the Presidents of the Church loved.

1. __ __ __ __ __
      2

2. __ __ __ __ __
      13   14

3. __ __ __ __
     1

4. __ __ __ __ __
          6

5. __ __ __ __ __
    12   5

6. __ __ __ __
     3

7. __ __ __
   4

8. __ __ __ __ __
            10

9. __ __ __ __ __
         7

10. __ __ __ __ __
    11

11. __ __ __ __
    8

12. __ __ __ __
    15

13. __ __ __ __ __
          9

__ __ __ __ __ __ __
1   2   3   4   5   6   7

__ __ __ __ __ __ __ __
8   9   10   11   12   13   14   15

18

Sacrament Prayers
D & C 20:77, 79

Advance Preparation

1. Marking pencils and personal copies of the Doctrine and Covenants.
2. Cut out the four copies of the splintered messages found at the end of this lesson.
3. Cut out game squares for the Know and Do game found at the end of this lesson.
4. Envelope containing numbered squares.
5. Paper and pencil for keeping score.

Activity: Splintered Messages

1. Divide the family into two, three, or four groups and give each group a pencil and a copy of the splintered messages. The groups should keep the messages face down until they are told to begin.

2. In the splintered messages, spaces between the letters have been reordered so that it is difficult to read the messages. (Example: "Living the gospel brings us happiness" might look like "Li vin gt hego spe lbri ngsu sha ppin e ss.")

3. When the signal is given, each team turns over their paper and proceeds to decipher the splintered messages. The correct messages should be written beneath the splintered ones. The team that finishes first and has all of the messages correct is the winner. All teams should be given a chance to finish before the correct answers are given. Teams could take turns reading the deciphered messages.

Here are the correct answers to the splintered messages:

- *All of us sin, and this ordinance gives us a chance to renew our baptismal covenants.*

- *If we keep the promises we make, God promises us his Spirit.*

- *We should be thinking of Jesus and of his wonderful atonement.*

- *During this time, we can evaluate our lives and promise to do better.*

4. Tell the family that all of the messages have to do with today's scriptures. Ask them to use these clues to guess the topic. (Sacrament prayers.)

Scripture

Have family members read the sacrament prayers found in Doctrine and Covenants 20:77, 79. Mark them if you haven't done it already. Discuss the importance of the sacrament and the sacrament prayers with your family. You may desire to use some of the following questions and ideas.

1. What are we to remember when we partake of the bread? (The body of Christ.)
2. When we remember the body of Christ, what do we think about? (His death and

125

resurrection and that we can be resurrected. That he was willing to suffer and give his life for us. That we can receive an immortal body because of Jesus.)

3. Have the family cross out the word *wine* and write in the word *water*. Have the family turn to Doctrine and Covenants 27:2–4, where the Lord said it doesn't matter what we use if our intentions are right and we have in mind what the sacrament is all about.

4. What are we to remember when we partake of the water? (The blood of Christ.)

5. When we remember the blood of Christ, what do we think about? (That he suffered for our sins in the Garden of Gethsemane to the extent that he bled from every pore. That we can be forgiven of our sins if we repent. Things we need to do to repent and take advantage of his atonement. We can also promise God that we will try to do these things and ask him to help us.)

6. Have the family read the blessing for the bread (verse 77) and identify the three promises we make when we partake of the sacrament. (Take his name upon us, always remember him, and keep his commandments.)

7. Briefly discuss these promises and what they mean, and then have family members identify what is promised us if we keep our promises. (That we will have the Lord's Spirit with us.) Can you think of any greater promise than having the protection, guidance, and comfort of God in our lives?

8. Commit the family to making the sacrament time a more meaningful experience in their lives.

Game: Know and Do

1. Place the game squares in two rows of nine on the floor or table.

2. Remove the numbers from the numbered squares envelope and place them in order from 1 through 18 on top of the game squares.

3. Divide the family into two, three, or four teams. Have team one remove any one of the number squares and reveal the game square underneath.

4. All of the game squares tell something that one team member or the whole team needs to do. They also show the number of points that the team will receive for doing the activity.

5. If the team cannot do what is called for, the number is placed back over the game square and another team will have a chance at it. If they do the activity, they should score the points and keep the card.

6. After team one has had their turn, team two will choose a number and play will continue. When all of the game squares have been removed, or no team can perform correctly the activities on any squares that are left, the game is over and the team with the most points is declared the winner.

Al lof ussi na ndth iso rdina nceg ive sus acha ncet oren ewo urba ptis ma lcov ena nts.

Ifw eke epth epro mis esw ema keg odpr omis esu shiss pi rit.

Wes ho ul dbet hin kin gofj esu san dofh isw ond er fula ton eme nt.

Du rin gth ist im ewec anev alu ate o url iv esa ndpr om iset odob ett er.

Al lof ussi na ndth iso rdina nceg ive sus acha ncet oren ewo urba ptis ma lcov ena nts.

Ifw eke epth epro mis esw ema keg odpr omis esu shiss pi rit.

Wes ho ul dbet hin kin gofj esu san dofh isw ond er fula ton eme nt.

Du rin gth ist im ewec anev alu ate o url iv esa ndpr om iset odob ett er.

Al lof ussi na ndth iso rdina nceg ive sus acha ncet oren ewo urba ptis ma lcov ena nts.

Ifw eke epth epro mis esw ema keg odpr omis esu shiss pi rit.

Wes ho ul dbet hin kin gofj esu san dofh isw ond er fula ton eme nt.

Du rin gth ist im ewec anev alu ate o url iv esa ndpr om iset odob ett er.

Al lof ussi na ndth iso rdina nceg ive sus acha ncet oren ewo urba ptis ma lcov ena nts.

Ifw eke epth epro mis esw ema keg odpr omis esu shiss pi rit.

Wes ho ul dbet hin kin gofj esu san dofh isw ond er fula ton eme nt.

Du rin gth ist im ewec anev alu ate o url iv esa ndpr om iset odob ett er.

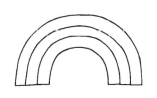

Everyone on team give
one good reason for
serving a mission.

15 points

One person share a
favorite scripture.

20 points

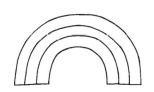

Everyone on the team share
one thing he or she has
learned about Church history.

25 points

Every person on team
name a favorite Book of
Mormon person and give a
reason for the choice.

25 points

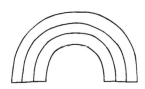

Sing a Christmas song of
your choice.

10 points

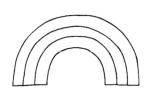

Share an embarrassing
moment with the family.

10 points

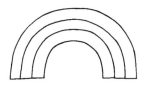

Name the first four
principles and
ordinances of the gospel.

15 points

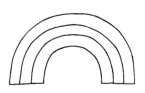

Give the references to four of
the key scriptures.

*5 points
for each reference*

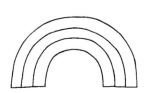

Give one of the
Articles of Faith almost
word perfect.

15 points

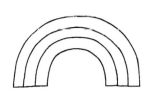

Give everyone not on your team a sincere compliment.

15 points

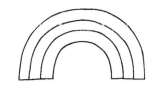

Have one person sincerely tell why he or she appreciates Jesus.

25 points

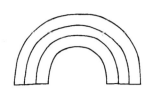

Everyone on team give one reason why he or she enjoys being a member of the family.

20 points

Everyone on team give one reason why he or she likes the bishop.

15 points

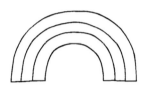

Give the names of the first six latter-day prophets in order.

*4 points
for each*

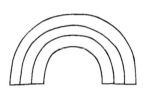

Sing "'Give,' Said the Little Stream."

10 points

Tell something special you remember another family member doing.

20 points

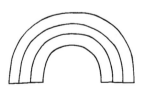

Tell a joke.

10 points

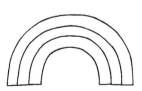

Everyone on team tell something that we can do to help our testimonies grow.

20 points

19

Family Scavenger Hunt

Advance Preparation

1. Cut out category cards found at the end of this lesson.
2. Cut out scavenger lists found at the end of this lesson.
3. Provide some bags for carrying items from the Family Scavenger Hunt. (If you prefer, provide pencils and instruct teams to leave items in place and simply make a check on the list when an item is found.)

Activity: Family Scavenger Hunt

1. Divide the family into three teams.
2. Give each team a scavenger list and instruct the teams to search in the house for the items on the list. Specify whether they should collect items in a bag or just check them off the list. There is a ten-minute limit. If they fail to return within the ten minutes, they must subtract one item for every minute they're late.
3. On the word *go,* each team begins to collect as many things on the list as they can, and returns to the room where family night is being held.
4. At the end of the ten minutes, each team receives one point for every item they found that was on their list. They also receive a bonus point for each item they found that has an asterisk (*) by it on the list. Remember to subtract one point for each late minute.
5. Place the category cards face down on the floor or the table.
6. One team begins by drawing one of the category cards. After reading the category, they choose one of the items found on the scavenger hunt and liken that item to the category and explain the connection. (For example, the category might be repentance and the item a Band-Aid. Repentance is like a Band-Aid because it helps us heal wounds.)
7. Play rotates from team to team until all of the category cards or all of the items have been used. An item can be used only once.
8. The team receives one point for every item they can liken to a category.

Scavenger List 1

Band-Aid

Pencil with an eraser

Blank piece of lined paper

Half-teaspoon measuring spoon

Piece of tinfoil

* Sock with a hole in it

Car keys

* Yellow toothbrush

Scotch tape

* Piece of Christmas wrapping paper

* Fifty-cent piece

Bottle of shampoo

* Slipper

Hairbrush

Broom

Scavenger List 2

Light bulb

White pillowcase

Can of soup

Toothpaste

Sewing needle

D encyclopedia

Piece of lined paper

Nail

Straight pin

White shirt

* Bookmark

* Red pencil

Ten-foot length of string

* Vacuum cleaner bag

* Fingernail file

Scavenger List 3

Black sock

* Belt buckle

* Fingernail clipper

Hammer

Tape measure

* Sunglasses

Shoe polish

Paper clip

Cassette tape

* Stapler

Bar of soap

Car keys

Five-dollar bill

Tube of lipstick

* Safety pin

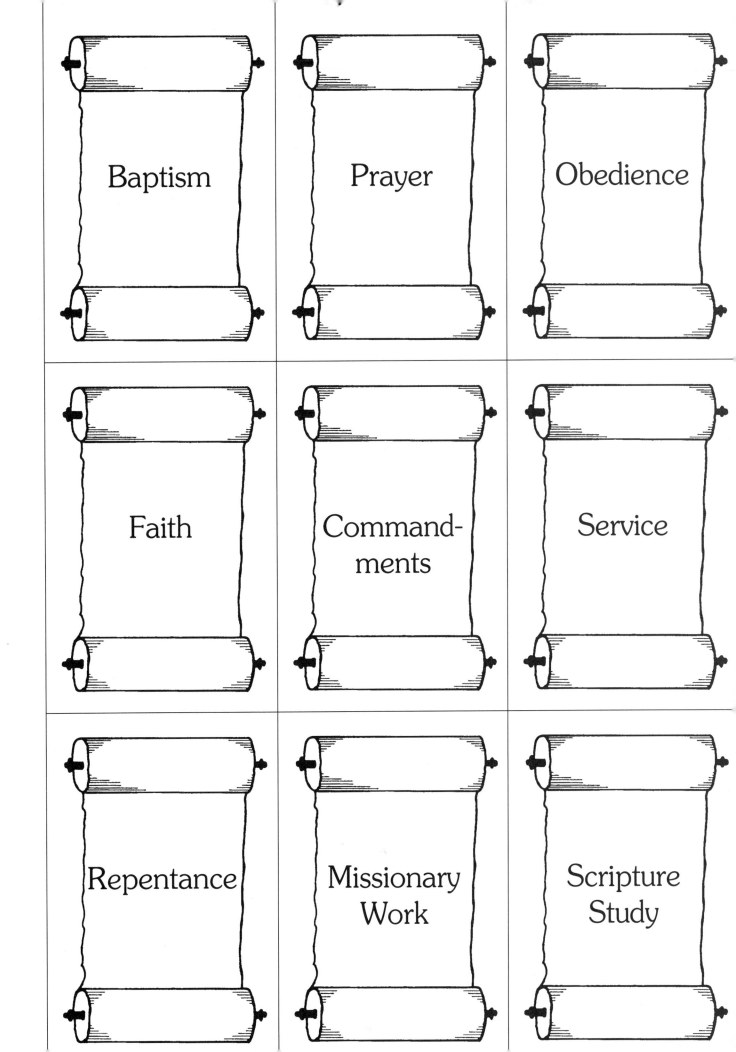

Baptism

Prayer

Obedience

Faith

Command-ments

Service

Repentance

Missionary Work

Scripture Study

20

Samuel Smith,
the First Missionary

Advance Preparation

1. Cut out the four copies of the Missionary Ladder found at the end of this lesson.
2. Four pencils for the Missionary Activity.
3. Cut out the Plates and Wagons game squares found at the end of the lesson and place them in an envelope.
4. Review the rules for Plates and Wagons game found in the chapter "Games for Many Occasions."
5. Become acquainted with the questions and suggestions found in chapters "Game Questions" and "Children's Questions."
6. Numbered squares envelope. Fifteen of the numbers will be used in the Plates and Wagons game.

Missionary Activity

Divide the family into four groups (or less, if necessary) and give each group a copy of the Missionary Ladder. Have each group fill in the correct answers.

When the groups have finished, take turns reading the ten statements about missionaries.

Tell the family that this lesson is about the first missionary called by the Church and ask them if they know who he was. (Samuel Smith, the younger brother of Joseph Smith.)

Story: Samuel Smith, the First Missionary

Samuel Smith was Joseph Smith's brother. He loved Joseph and knew that he was a prophet of God. He also knew that the Book of Mormon was true. Samuel had been one of the witnesses who had been allowed to see and feel the gold plates. He must have felt very special and excited as he turned the leaves of the sacred plates.

Samuel had a strong desire to preach the gospel, and the Lord called him to be the first missionary sent out by the restored Church. He was called to go to northern New York. He filled a backpack full of copies of the Book of Mormon and started off on his mission.

Samuel did a lot of walking; in fact he walked twenty-five miles the first day. He talked to a lot of people along the way, but no one wanted to buy or read the Book of Mormon. He was tired and hungry, and finally came to a large inn.

Samuel entered the inn to see if he could sell a copy of the Book of Mormon. When he told the innkeeper that the book was translated from gold plates that had been buried in the ground, the man called him a liar and turned him out of the inn.

Samuel felt very discouraged. He walked another five miles down the road until he came to a large apple tree. He spent the night trying to sleep there on the cold, hard ground.

By the time Samuel woke up the next morning he was really hungry. A poor widow felt sorry for Samuel and invited him into her house, where she fed him a good breakfast. Samuel gave her a Book of Mormon in payment for his meal and knew she would be converted if she read it with a prayerful heart.

Samuel left the widow's home and walked eight miles until he came to the home of John P. Greene, who was a Methodist minister. Mr. Greene was not interested in reading the Book of Mormon, but he agreed to see if any of his friends might be interested in it, so Samuel left a copy with him. Upon returning to Mr. Greene's three weeks later, Samuel found that no one had wanted the book, but Mr. Greene's wife, Rhoda, had read it and was convinced that it was true. Later she talked her husband into reading it, and he was converted also. Both were baptized into the Church.

Samuel continued on his mission until all of his books were gone. Early in that mission one of the books had been purchased by a man named Phinehas Young. This book was passed around to his family and friends, and several of them were converted to the Church from this one book alone. Included in those who were converted were Brigham Young and Heber C. Kimball. Brigham Young became the second President of the Church and brought the pioneers across the plains. Heber C. Kimball was a counselor to Brigham Young and the grandfather of Spencer W. Kimball, who became a President of the Church.

Sometimes one mission and two books can be very important. Your mission will be very important to many people also.

Game: Plates and Wagons

1. Play Plates and Wagons (see instructions for the game in the chapter "Games for Many Occasions").

2. Use the questions from lessons 1 through 20 found in the chapter "Game Questions." If you have younger children, you can also use questions from the chapter "Children's Questions."

Note: When you are through playing the game, save the game squares in an envelope marked "Plates and Wagons" so they can be used again.

Missionary Ladder

Climb the ladder by writing the correct word on each step.

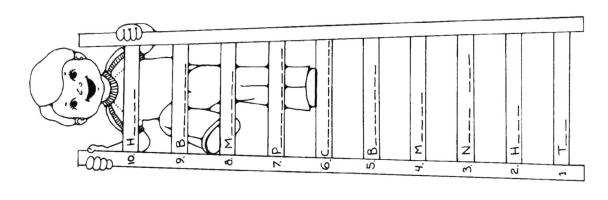

10. Missionaries like to tell people about the Church because it makes them _____ .

9. Missionaries teach people about the Church and _____ them.

8. Missionaries tell people about the Book of _____ .

7. When a person is called on a mission, he or she gets a letter from the _____ of the Church.

6. A person who goes on a mission needs to be keeping the _____ .

5. A lot of missionaries ride _____ .

4. It costs a lot of _____ to go on a mission.

3. Missionaries always wear a _____ .

2. Before a young man goes on a mission, he needs to have a short _____ cut.

1. How many missionaries normally make up a companionship?

Missionary Ladder

Climb the ladder by writing the correct word on each step.

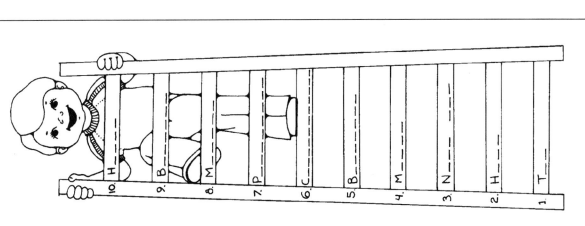

10. Missionaries like to tell people about the Church because it makes them _____ .

9. Missionaries teach people about the Church and _____ them.

8. Missionaries tell people about the Book of _____ .

7. When a person is called on a mission, he or she gets a letter from the _____ of the Church.

6. A person who goes on a mission needs to be keeping the _____ .

5. A lot of missionaries ride _____ .

4. It costs a lot of _____ to go on a mission.

3. Missionaries always wear a _____ .

2. Before a young man goes on a mission, he needs to have a short _____ cut.

1. How many missionaries normally make up a companionship?

Missionary Ladder

Climb the ladder by writing the correct word on each step.

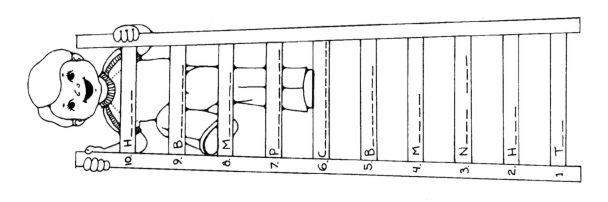

10. Missionaries like to tell people about the Church because it makes them _____.

9. Missionaries teach people about the Church and _____ them.

8. Missionaries tell people about the Book of _____.

7. When a person is called on a mission, he or she gets a letter from the _____ of the Church.

6. A person who goes on a mission needs to be keeping the _____.

5. A lot of missionaries ride _____.

4. It costs a lot of _____ to go on a mission.

3. Missionaries always wear a _____.

2. Before a young man goes on a mission, he needs to have a short _____ cut.

1. How many missionaries normally make up a companionship?

Missionary Ladder

Climb the ladder by writing the correct word on each step.

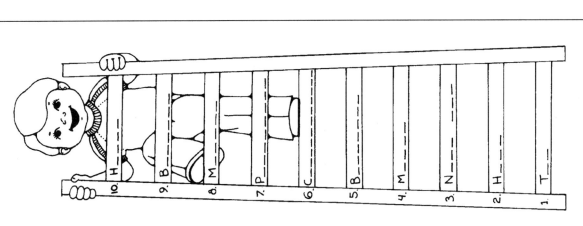

10. Missionaries like to tell people about the Church because it makes them _____.

9. Missionaries teach people about the Church and _____ them.

8. Missionaries tell people about the Book of _____.

7. When a person is called on a mission, he or she gets a letter from the _____ of the Church.

6. A person who goes on a mission needs to be keeping the _____.

5. A lot of missionaries ride _____.

4. It costs a lot of _____ to go on a mission.

3. Missionaries always wear a _____.

2. Before a young man goes on a mission, he needs to have a short _____ cut.

1. How many missionaries normally make up a companionship?

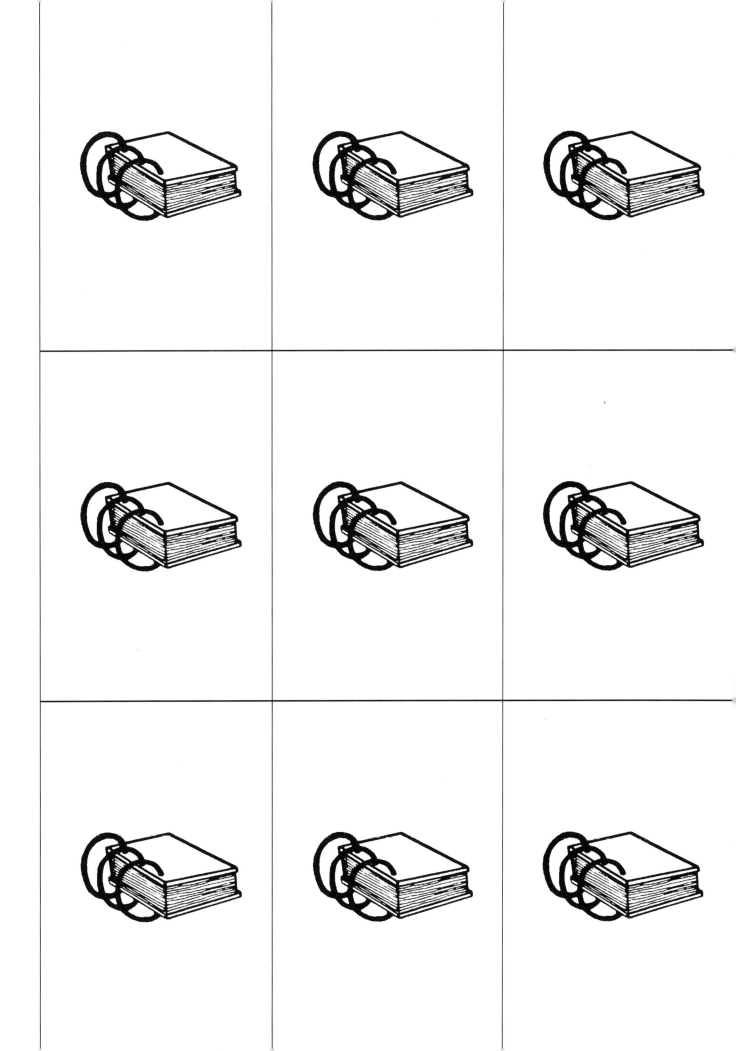

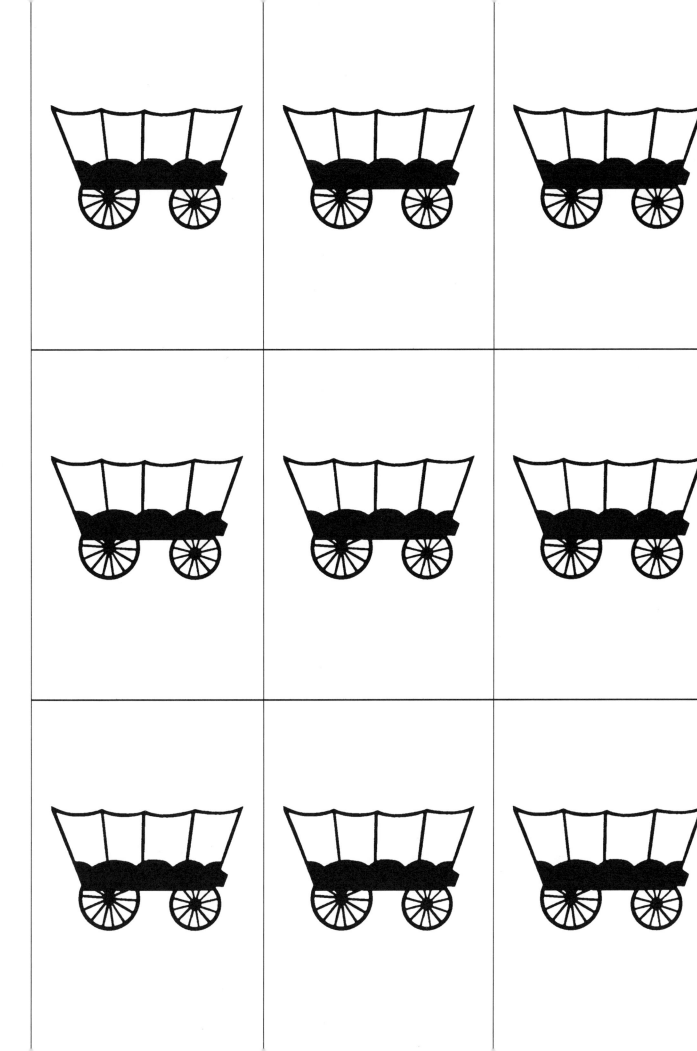

21

Making an Eternal Family

Advance Preparation

1. A doughnut for each member of the family. Use only one in the first part of the activity. Save the others for a surprise ending.
2. Review the rules for High-Low found in the chapter "Games for Many Occasions."
3. Review the instructions for I've Got a Question found in the chapter "Key Scripture Ideas."
4. A pencil or pen and a piece of paper for each family member.

Activity

1. Give everyone a pencil or pen and a piece of paper.

2. Show the family *one* doughnut and ask who would like to eat it. If more than one person volunteers, play High-Low (found in the chapter "Games for Many Occasions") using the list of the Presidents of the Church to determine who gets to eat it.

3. Tell the chosen person that, before he can eat the doughnut, he must first name all of the things a doughnut is made of. When the person finishes, have everyone else write down anything they think the person may have missed. After everyone is through writing, have all family members share what they wrote down.

4. Next, have the person describe how to make a doughnut. When he is done, have everyone else write down anything they think the person may have missed. After everyone is through writing, have all family members share what they wrote down.

5. Explain to everyone that a doughnut can be likened to an eternal family. Just having all the ingredients doesn't make a doughnut. You have to mix and cook the ingredients properly to get a doughnut. Likewise, a group of people living together doesn't necessarily make an eternal family. You also have to do the things necessary to make them work together. As a family, name some things you could do to make an eternal family.

6. Point out to the family that the doughnut's ring is a symbol of eternity—it has no end. So it is with an eternal family—it has no end. Cut the doughnut into several pieces and point out that, even though you can make a doughnut, if you don't take care of it, it can be destroyed. The same holds true with the family. As a family, name all the things you can think of that will help you preserve an eternal family.

7. Give everyone a doughnut.

Key Scripture Review

Play I've Got a Question (instructions are found in the chapter "Key Scripture Ideas").

22

Remember Sins No More
D & C 58:42–43

Advance Preparation

1. Marking pencils and individual copies of the Doctrine and Covenants.
2. Become acquainted with the meaning of the key words found in Doctrine and Covenants 58:42-43. (For some possible help, see steps 4 and 5 under the heading "Scripture" in this lesson.)
3. Pencils and paper for playing the Square Game.
4. Study the Square Game rules found in the chapter "Games for Many Occasions." Cut out the game pieces for the Square Game found at the end of this lesson.

Activity: Count Your Blessings

1. A knowledge of the alphabet and words is necessary to play this activity, so younger children need to be paired with older family members. The two can work together, and the younger child can always give the answer.

2. Family members are seated around the room or in a circle. One person should be a timer and call "time" if ten seconds go by without an acceptable response. The first player starts off by saying, "I am grateful for apples"—or something else that begins with the letter A.

3. The next family member names something she is grateful for that starts with the letter B, such as, "I am grateful for basketball."

4. The next player uses a C word, and so on through the alphabet. If a family member fails to think of an acceptable word within ten seconds, he or she drops out of the game.

5. There are two different ways that the game can end. Play can continue until only one person is left (when Z is reached just start over at A). The other method of play is to declare winners all those who are still in the game when the family gets through the alphabet. If family members choose to go through the alphabet more than once, let them know that no word can be used twice.

Scripture

1. Tell the family that today's scripture discusses something of great worth that we should feel eternally grateful for. This is the wonderful gift of repentance and forgiveness.

2. Have each member of the family turn to Doctrine and Covenants 58:42–43. Mark it if you haven't done so already.

3. Keep the pairing you used in the preceding activity. Have each group read the scripture to themselves and circle the four most important words in each of the two verses (eight words total).

4. Have family members share what they felt were the most important words and ask them to define each of them. They will probably include such words as *repented, sins, forgiven, remember, confess,* and *forsake.*

5. Here are some ideas concerning these key words that may be helpful to you. (This is a good opportunity to use the LDS Bible Dictionary.)

Repented, Repenteth: Repentance is more than stopping wrong behavior. It is "a turning of the heart and will to God." It is desiring to do whatever God wants us to do. (See LDS Bible Dictionary, pp. 760-61.)

Sins: We sin when we do what we shouldn't do, or when we don't do what we should do. Sometimes it is just as wrong not to do something right as it is to do something wrong.

Forgiven: When we are truly repentant, God pardons our sins. This means that we will not have to suffer for them, because Jesus suffered in our place.

Remember: In this case God is saying that, because we are truly repentant, he will never refer to our sins or bring them up in any way. As far as he is concerned, they are forgotten.

Confess: The first step in repentance is confessing, admitting to ourselves that we have sinned. We also need to confess our sins to our Father in Heaven in prayer, and ask him to help us overcome them. Serious sins, usually those dealing with immorality, also need to be confessed to God's representatives on the earth (bishops). (See LDS Bible Dictionary, p. 649.)

Forsake: To forsake sin is to abandon or leave our sinful way of life and try to live the way God wants us to live.

The Square Game

1. Divide the family into two, three, or four teams.

2. Read aloud the instructions for playing the game. These are found in the chapter "Games for Many Occasions." Use the game pieces found at the end of this lesson.

3. Use the questions from lessons 1 through 22 found in the "Game Questions" chapter. If young children are involved, also use the questions from the chapter "Children's Questions."

4. When the game is finished, save the twenty-five game markers in an envelope marked "The Square Game." It would be easy to draw the game grids and play the game again at a future date.

★	A	B	C	D	E
1					
2					
3					
4					
5					

A1	A2	A3	A4	A5
B1	B2	B3	B4	B5
C1	C2	C3	C4	C5
D1	D2	D3	D4	D5
E1	E2	E3	E4	E5

Smile	10 pts.
Gold Plates	20 pts.
Covered Wagon	30 pts.
Savior	40 pts.
Frown	-10 pts.
Bomb	-20 pts.
Cigar	-30 pts.
Devil	-40 pts.
Star	+5 or -5 pts.

★	A	B	C	D	E
1					
2					
3					
4					
5					

Smile	10 pts.
Gold Plates	20 pts.
Covered Wagon	30 pts.
Savior	40 pts.
Frown	-10 pts.
Bomb	-20 pts.
Cigar	-30 pts.
Devil	-40 pts.
Star	+5 or -5 pts.

★	A	B	C	D	E
1					
2					
3					
4					
5					

Smile	10 pts.
Gold Plates	20 pts.
Covered Wagon	30 pts.
Savior	40 pts.
Frown	-10 pts.
Bomb	-20 pts.
Cigar	-30 pts.
Devil	-40 pts.
Star	+5 or -5 pts.

★	A	B	C	D	E
1					
2					
3					
4					
5					

Smile	10 pts.
Gold Plates	20 pts.
Covered Wagon	30 pts.
Savior	40 pts.
Frown	-10 pts.
Bomb	-20 pts.
Cigar	-30 pts.
Devil	-40 pts.
Star	+5 or -5 pts.

★	A	B	C	D	E
1					
2					
3					
4					
5					

Smile	10 pts.
Gold Plates	20 pts.
Covered Wagon	30 pts.
Savior	40 pts.
Frown	-10 pts.
Bomb	-20 pts.
Cigar	-30 pts.
Devil	-40 pts.
Star	+5 or -5 pts.

23

For God's Work

Advance Preparation

1   A piece of paper and pencil or pen for each member of the family.
2.   Key Scripture bookmarks (from lesson 5).
3.   Review rules for High-Low found in the chapter "Games for Many Occasions."
4.   Cut out the year cards found at the end of this lesson.
5.   Review rules for Three Up found in the chapter "Key Scripture Ideas."

Activity

1.   Give each family member a piece of paper and a pencil or pen.
2.   Have each family member make a paper airplane out of his or her piece of paper.
3.   Have everyone write the name of his or her airplane on the wings. The name should have something to do with one of the key scriptures. (For example, a plane could be named "Search 1" in connection with D&C 1:37–38, or "The Spirit of Revelation" in connection with D&C 8:2–3, etc.)
4.   After everyone has completed an airplane, awards could be given for best name, slickest design, most practical, and so on. The planes could be judged by having each family member vote by secret ballot.
5.   Then the family can go outside, weather permitting, and see whose plane will fly the farthest. Each person has five flights to determine his or her plane's longest distance.
6.   Using the High-Low method, have the family guess what year the Wright Brothers made their first sustained flight (1903). Ask what had to happen to accomplish such a feat. Guide the family so that they discuss what God has given us. God gives us knowledge and opportunities for great inventions, such as the airplane. Ask the family to name all of the ways they can think of that the airplane has benefited the work of God. Point out to the family that knowledge has greatly increased since the gospel was restored through the Prophet Joseph Smith. Many of the greatest inventions in the history of the earth have happened in the last century. These inventions have helped in many ways in furthering God's work throughout the earth.

Game

1.   Place the year cards face down on the floor or table.
2.   Divide the family into two or three teams, depending on the size of your family.
3.   Begin by having one of the teams turn over one of the year cards. They then have thirty seconds to name two things that were invented after that year. They receive one point for naming the invention and two bonus points if they can tell how it has benefited the work of God. Play then rotates to the next team and continues until all of the year cards have been turned over. The parents should determine if the answers are correct. If there is a question, the item could be looked up in an encyclopedia.

Game

1. Divide the family into two teams, all of the children on one team and the parents on the other team.

2. Each team has three minutes to write down everything that they can think of that has been invented since the parents were children.

3. At the end of the three minutes, each team will read their list and receive one point for every item that is correct and two bonus points for every item that the other team didn't have on their list.

Activity

1. Give each family member five minutes to think of some future invention that would benefit the work of God.

2. At the end of the five minutes have each family member discuss his or her invention.

3. Conclude by pointing out to the family that we should thank Heavenly Father daily for the great things he has given us to help him with his work.

Key Scripture Review

Play Three Up (rules are found in the chapter "Key Scripture Ideas").

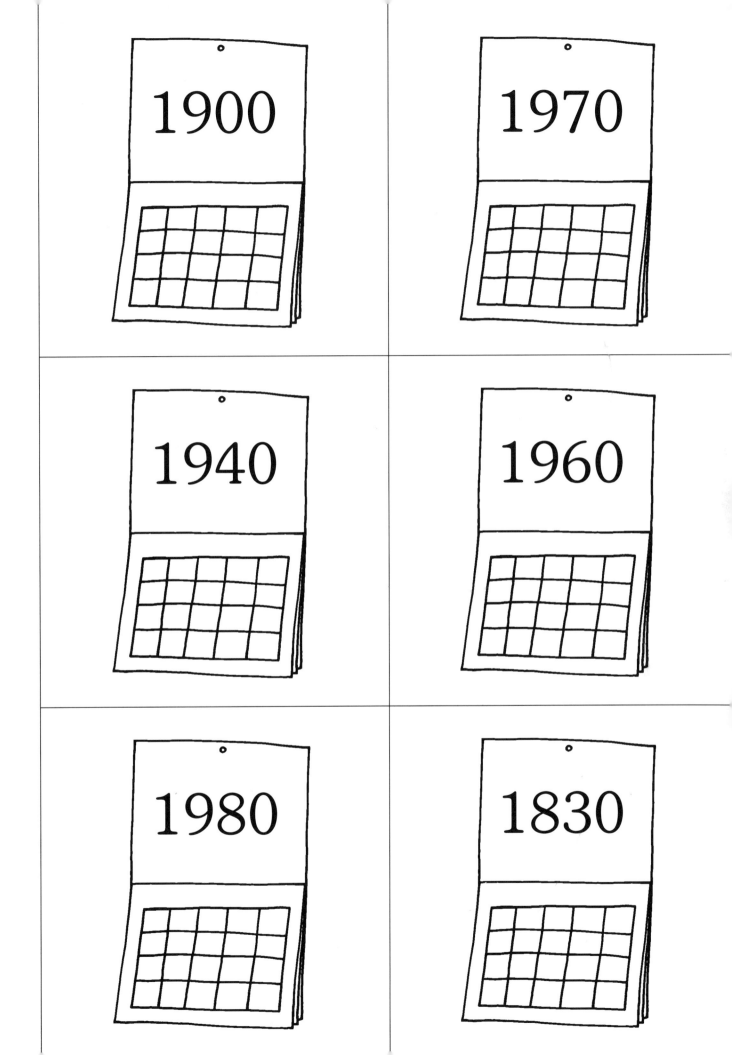

24

Wilford Woodruff
in England

Advance Preparation

1. Cut out the four copies of "Wilford Woodruff's Accidents" found at the end of this lesson.
2. Cut out the four sets of ten words and place the sets in separate envelopes.
3. At least four pencils, one for each group.
4. Review rules for Stack It game found in the chapter "Games for Many Occasions" and get a set of children's blocks, preferably one with different shapes and sizes.

Activity: Wilford's Accidents

1. Divide the family into no more than four groups and give each group a copy of "Wilford Woodruff's Accidents."

2. Give each group an envelope containing the ten words. They cannot look at the words until the signal is given.

3. Explain to the family that Wilford Woodruff was the fourth President of the Church and that Heavenly Father helped him survive a number of life-threatening events before he became the prophet. Each group has a list of ten of the accidents that Wilford Woodruff suffered while growing up. In the envelope are the ten words that fit in the blanks.

4. On the word *go,* each group is to remove the words from the envelope, decide which sentences the words fit in, and write the words in the correct sentences. The first group to *correctly* complete the sheet will be the winner.

5. When all of the groups have finished, have them take turns reading the statements. Make sure that the correct words have been written in. The correct words are:

1. water	4. overturned	7. foot
2. face	5. drowned	8. broke
3. pumpkin	6. death	9. ox
		10. hay

Story

As you can see, the Lord helped and protected Wilford Woodruff many times so he could live to become a prophet. Even before he became President of the Church he did many great things. One of the most important of these was his mission to England.

Five years after the Church was organized, it had grown to several thousand members. On the Lord's instructions, in 1835 Joseph set up a quorum of twelve Apostles. In 1838 the Lord selected Wilford Woodruff to fill one of the vacancies in the quorum. He also directed Joseph Smith to send the Apostles on missions to England.

Wilford Woodruff and John Taylor were the first two Apostles to leave for England. The morning they left, Elder Woodruff was so sick that he lay down to rest after traveling only a short distance from his home. When Joseph Smith saw him lying there, he told him to get up and continue on his mission and promised him that everything would go well with him. Wilford obeyed.

Wilford Woodruff was a powerful missionary because he lived so that the Spirit of the Lord could be with him. The following story shows the kind of thing that can happen when we preach with the power of the Holy Ghost.

Elder Woodruff had baptized a man named John Benbow. He set up a meeting in Brother Benbow's house, but as he got up to speak to the assembled people, a man came into the room. He said that he was a policeman sent by the minister of the local church to arrest Elder Woodruff for preaching to the people.

Elder Woodruff told him that he had a license to preach, just as the minister had. He asked the policeman to sit down and promised him that he would talk with him immediately after the meeting.

Elder Woodruff then gave a powerful talk on the principles of the gospel, which lasted over an hour. The power of God was present and the room was filled with his Spirit. When Elder Woodruff closed the meeting, seven people asked to be baptized. Four of them were preachers; and one of the other three was the policeman who had come to arrest Elder Woodruff.

After seven had been baptized, the policeman went back to the minister who had sent him and told him, "If you want Mr. Woodruff arrested, then you must serve the papers on him yourself. Mr. Woodruff preached the only true sermon I have heard in my life."

The minister didn't know what to make of all this, so he sent two of his clerks to spy on the meetings and find out what was being preached. They were both converted and baptized into the Church. The minister became very worried and decided not to send anyone else to the meetings.

With the great spirit that Wilford Woodruff had, he was able to baptize hundreds of British people into the Church. He carried the same spirit with him throughout his life.

Game: Stack It

Using the questions from the first twenty-four lessons (found in the chapter "Game Questions") and the questions found in the chapter "Children's Questions," play the game Stack It (the rules are found in the chapter "Games for Many Occasions").

Your family has now played many games during the year, and you may have developed some family favorites. Don't hesitate to substitute favorite games for games that are suggested in the lessons.

Wilford Woodruff's Accidents

1. When he was three years old, he fell into a big pot of boiling _____ and was burned so badly that it took nine months to get better.

2. At age six he fell from the top of the barn to the hard ground right on his _____ .

3. While being chased by a bull, Wilford tripped and fell down. The bull jumped over him and tore into pieces the _____ that Wilford had been carrying.

4. When he was eight, the wagon he was on was wrecked when the horse got scared, ran down a hill, and _____ the wagon.

5. At age twelve he nearly _____ , but Heavenly Father sent a man to save him.

6. At age thirteen he almost froze to _____ .

7. When he was fourteen he hit his foot with an ax while chopping wood and nearly chopped off his _____ .

8. When he was seventeen his horse went crazy, ran down a steep hill, and threw him over his head onto some rocks. Wilford could have been killed but only _____ his leg.

9. Many other accidents happened to Wilford, including being kicked by an _____ .

10. He almost smothered to death the day a huge pile of _____ fell on him.

Wilford Woodruff's Accidents

1. When he was three years old, he fell into a big pot of boiling _____ and was burned so badly that it took nine months to get better.

2. At age six he fell from the top of the barn to the hard ground right on his _____ .

3. While being chased by a bull, Wilford tripped and fell down. The bull jumped over him and tore into pieces the _____ that Wilford had been carrying.

4. When he was eight, the wagon he was on was wrecked when the horse got scared, ran down a hill, and _____ the wagon.

5. At age twelve he nearly _____ , but Heavenly Father sent a man to save him.

6. At age thirteen he almost froze to _____ .

7. When he was fourteen he hit his foot with an ax while chopping wood and nearly chopped off his _____ .

8. When he was seventeen his horse went crazy, ran down a steep hill, and threw him over his head onto some rocks. Wilford could have been killed but only _____ his leg.

9. Many other accidents happened to Wilford, including being kicked by an _____ .

10. He almost smothered to death the day a huge pile of _____ fell on him.

Wilford Woodruff's Accidents

1. When he was three years old, he fell into a big pot of boiling _____ and was burned so badly that it took nine months to get better.

2. At age six he fell from the top of the barn to the hard ground right on his _____ .

3. While being chased by a bull, Wilford tripped and fell down. The bull jumped over him and tore into pieces the _____ that Wilford had been carrying.

4. When he was eight, the wagon he was on was wrecked when the horse got scared, ran down a hill, and _____ the wagon.

5. At age twelve he nearly _____ , but Heavenly Father sent a man to save him.

6. At age thirteen he almost froze to _____ .

7. When he was fourteen he hit his foot with an ax while chopping wood and nearly chopped off his _____ .

8. When he was seventeen his horse went crazy, ran down a steep hill, and threw him over his head onto some rocks. Wilford could have been killed but only _____ his leg.

9. Many other accidents happened to Wilford, including being kicked by an _____ .

10. He almost smothered to death the day a huge pile of _____ fell on him.

Wilford Woodruff's Accidents

1. When he was three years old, he fell into a big pot of boiling _____ and was burned so badly that it took nine months to get better.

2. At age six he fell from the top of the barn to the hard ground right on his _____ .

3. While being chased by a bull, Wilford tripped and fell down. The bull jumped over him and tore into pieces the _____ that Wilford had been carrying.

4. When he was eight, the wagon he was on was wrecked when the horse got scared, ran down a hill, and _____ the wagon.

5. At age twelve he nearly _____ , but Heavenly Father sent a man to save him.

6. At age thirteen he almost froze to _____ .

7. When he was fourteen he hit his foot with an ax while chopping wood and nearly chopped off his _____ .

8. When he was seventeen his horse went crazy, ran down a steep hill, and threw him over his head onto some rocks. Wilford could have been killed but only _____ his leg.

9. Many other accidents happened to Wilford, including being kicked by an _____ .

10. He almost smothered to death the day a huge pile of _____ fell on him.

water	face
foot	pumpkin
broke	overturned
ox	drowned
hay	death
water	face
foot	pumpkin
broke	overturned
ox	drowned
hay	death

water	face
foot	pumpkin
broke	overturned
ox	drowned
hay	death
water	face
foot	pumpkin
broke	overturned
ox	drowned
hay	death

25

The Lord's Day
D & C 59

Advance Preparation

1. Obtain five coins or washers for each family member.
2. Masking tape.
3. Pencils and paper for the Can Do activity.
4. Marking pencils and personal copies of the Doctrine and Covenants.
5. Study the rules for the Twenty-One game found in the chapter "Games for Many Occasions." Cut out the forty numbers for the Twenty-One game found at the end of this lesson and place them in a bowl or pan. Be sure to put them in an envelope labeled "Twenty-One" after playing the game.

Activity: The Closer the Better

1. Make a line on the floor with tape and give each family member five coins or washers.
2. Have each family member toss a coin at the line while standing approximately five feet from the line.
3. The person who tosses his coin nearest to the line wins all of the coins tossed during that turn.
4. Continue taking turns tossing coins until one person has won all of the coins and is declared the winner. If this doesn't take long, you could play it again.

Scripture Readiness Activity

Tell your family that there are great lessons to be learned from the coin toss activity, and ask them to think of some things the activity can teach. (One is that the closer we get to doing all that Heavenly Father wants us to do—that is, the more we keep ourselves firmly on the "strait and narrow path"—the more blessings we will receive.)

Tonight's topic is one of God's commandments. He promises us great blessings as we strive to live it fully. Ask family members to guess the topic from the following clues:

1. It helps us overcome sin.
2. It helps us worship the Lord and show him that we love him.
3. It gives us time to serve the Lord better.
4. If we obey this commandment properly we are promised that our joy will be full.
5. If we properly obey this commandment, we are promised that the good things of the earth will be ours.
6. We can learn about this commandment in section 59 of the Doctrine and Covenants.

Scripture

Have the family turn to section 59 in the Doctrine and Covenants to find out how they can receive the five blessings mentioned above. It would be good to have the family mark some of the more important phrases found between verse 9 and the end of the section. Here are some ideas you may desire to use:

1. *"Keep thyself unspotted from the world"* (v. 9)—Spots, of course, represent sins, and the Sabbath can help us develop strength to overcome the temptations that we face.

2. *"Rest from your labors, . . . pay thy devotions unto the Most High"* (v. 10)—It is not just a day of rest but a day of rest from our everyday labors. To receive the blessings of the Sabbath, our time needs to be spent in doing things that show devotion to God.

3. Verse 11 points out that we should be righteous every day, not just one day a week.

4. *"Offer thine oblations . . . unto the Most High"* (v. 12)—Footnote 12b in the 1981 edition of the Doctrine and Covenants says that *oblations* are "offerings, whether of time, talents, or means, in service of God and fellowman." The Sabbath is a day of service.

5. Verses 16–20 indicate that the fulness of the earth is made available to those who strive to keep the Sabbath holy as well as to obey the other commandments of God.

6. Verse 23 promises us that righteousness brings "peace in this world, and eternal life in the world to come."

Activity: Can Do

Too many of us spend too much time worrying about what we *can't do* on the Sabbath when we should be looking for all of the things that we *can do* on this holy day.

1. Divide the family into three groups. Give each group a pencil and paper and ten minutes to see how many things they can think of that would be appropriate to do on the Sabbath day.

2. Then have the groups take turns reading, one at a time, the things they have written down. No activity can be mentioned twice, so teams should check off of their lists any activity mentioned.

3. The group that still has activities left on their paper when the other groups have run out is declared the "Can Doers" of the family.

Here is a sample list of twenty activities that may be appropriate for the Sabbath:

1. Write letters to missionaries, grandparents, friends, etc.
2. Read the scriptures, Church magazines, and other uplifting materials.
3. Have family home evening.
4. Play gospel games as a family.
5. Prepare lessons and work on other Church materials.
6. Visit family members or shut-ins, widows, elderly neighbors, lonely people, etc.
7. Prepare an inspirational program. Visit some of the people mentioned in idea number 6 above and present the program to them.
8. Write in a journal, or do other family history work.
9. Sing songs together and have family talent shows.
10. Do home teaching and visiting teaching.
11. Attend Church meetings, including special broadcasts and firesides.
12. Share lessons taught at church.
13. Look at family pictures, slides, or movies.
14. Take gifts to those who are sick.
15. Study the lives and teachings of the prophets.
16. Hold family council meetings.
17. Read with the younger children.
18. Hold interviews with family members.
19. Visit the temple grounds.
20. Watch uplifting videos, movies, etc.

Church leaders have counseled that we should not fill the Sabbath so full of extra meetings that there is no time for prayer, meditation, family fellowship, and counseling.

Game: Twenty-One

Play Twenty-One (instructions are found in the chapter "Games for Many Occasions"), using any of the questions from lessons 1 through 25. The children's questions found at the back of the book can be used also.

1	1	1	1	2
2	2	2	3	3
3	3	4	4	4
4	5	5	5	5
6	6	6	6	7
7	7	7	8	8
8	8	9	9	9
9	10	10	10	10

26

Be of Good Cheer

D & C 61:36–37

Advance Preparation

1. Pencil or pen and drawing paper for each family member.
2. Copies of the Book of Mormon and the Doctrine and Covenants for each family member.
3. Review game rules for "Get the Picture?" found in the chapter "Games for Many Occasions." Cut out the four puzzles found at the end of this lesson and put them in separate envelopes.

Activity: Without the Light

1. Give each family member a pencil or pen and a piece of paper.
2. Turn out the lights and have all family members close their eyes. Tell them that peeking will not be allowed.
3. Have everyone draw a picture of a beautiful lake with mountains in the background and trees around the edge of the lake. Tell everyone to draw a boat on the lake with members of your family in it. Tell them to do the best they can with their eyes closed.
4. When they are finished, turn the lights on and have them share their handiwork. Chances are the pictures will be barely recognizable.
5. Have them turn their papers over and draw the same picture again, this time with the lights on and their eyes open. Compare these to the first drawings.

Tell the family that drawing in the dark is like trying to go through life without the help of the light and direction that Jesus gives us. We get a distorted picture of life and the things we should do are never quite clear to us.

Scripture

Explain that the scripture in this lesson gives two reasons why we should be happy (be of good cheer). Have the family guess what these reasons are. They will probably give many reasons for being happy. Agree, but do not, at this point, tell them whether or not they have guessed the reasons given in the scripture.

When they are through guessing, tell them to turn to Doctrine and Covenants 61:36–37 to see if they guessed the reasons given there. The two reasons given are wonderful ones that we sometimes don't think about. Discuss the two reasons with the family. Some of the following ideas may be helpful:

1. *Jesus is in our midst;* that is, he is with us and has not given up on us. Sometimes, when we are experiencing bad times or facing difficult decisions, we may feel alone, but this scripture gives us hope. As in the drawing activity, we can have the light that Jesus can give us to comfort and direct us if we accept his help and reach out to him. He is already reaching out to us.

2. Jesus promises us *the blessings of the kingdom* if we humble ourselves and follow

183

his teachings and promptings. Even though we may have problems to deal with here, he wants us to look ahead to the blessings available to us in this life and in the hereafter, and he wants us to be of good cheer. His light can help us see the complete picture of eternity, not just the limited picture of today.

The following game will guide the family to other scriptures that teach that Jesus wants us to be happy now and enjoy life in spite of the difficulties that we face.

Game: "Get the Picture?"

Play "Get the Picture?" (The rules are found in the chapter "Games for Many Occasions.") The game will be more fun if family members have their own scriptures. Here are the answers to the questions on the puzzle pieces:

2 Nephi 10:23	act for yourselves
Mosiah 2:41	blessed, happy
Alma 4:14	resurrection
Alma 41:10	wickedness, happiness
D&C 18:13	joy, repenteth
D&C 18:16	many souls
D&C 59:15-16	thanksgiving, hearts, countenances
D&C 68:6	stand by you
D&C 78:18	lead you along
D&C 112:4	ends of the earth

Mosiah 2:41

"Ye should consider on the _____ and _____ state of those that keep the commandments of God"

Alma 4:14

"Being filled with great joy because of the _____ of the dead"

D&C 78:18

"Be of good cheer, for I will _____ _____ _____"

D&C 68:6

"Be of good cheer, and do not fear, for I the Lord am with you, and will _____ _____"

Alma 41:10

"Behold, I say unto you, _____ never was _____"

D&C 112:4

"Be of good cheer . . . and thou shalt send forth my word unto the _____ _____ _____"

2 Nephi 10:23

"Cheer up your hearts, and remember that ye are free to _____ _____ _____"

D&C 59:15–16

"Inasmuch as ye do these things with _____, with cheerful _____ and _____, . . . the fulness of the earth is yours"

D&C 18:16

"How great will be your joy if you should bring _____ _____ unto me [Jesus]"

D&C 18:13

"How great is his [Jesus'] _____ in the soul that _____ _____"

Alma 4:14

"Being filled with great joy because of the _____ of the dead"

Mosiah 2:41

"Ye should consider on the _____ and _____ state of those that keep the commandments of God"

D&C 78:18

"Be of good cheer, for I will _____ _____ _____ _____"

D&C 68:6

"Be of good cheer, and do not fear, for I the Lord am with you, and will _____ _____"

Alma 41:10

"Behold, I say unto you, _____ never was _____"

D&C 112:4

"Be of good cheer . . . and thou shalt send forth my word unto the _____ _____"

2 Nephi 10:23

"Cheer up your hearts, and remember that ye are free to _____ _____"

D&C 59:15–16

"Inasmuch as ye do these things with _____, with cheerful _____ and _____ . . . the fulness of the earth is yours"

D&C 18:16

"How great will be your joy if you should bring _____ unto me [Jesus]"

D&C 18:13

"How great is his [Jesus'] _____ in the soul that _____"

Mosiah 2:41

"Ye should consider on the _____ and _____ state of those that keep the commandments of God"

Alma 4:14

"Being filled with great joy because of the _____ of the dead"

D&C 78:18

"Be of good cheer, for I will _____ _____ _____"

D&C 68:6

"Be of good cheer, and do not fear, for I the Lord am with you, and will _____ _____"

Alma 41:10

"Behold, I say unto you, _____ never was _____"

D&C 112:4

"Be of good cheer . . . and thou shalt send forth my word unto the _____ _____"

2 Nephi 10:23

"Cheer up your hearts, and remember that ye are free to _____ _____"

D&C 59:15–16

"Inasmuch as ye do these things with _____, with cheerful _____, and _____ . . . the fulness of the earth is yours"

D&C 18:16

"How great will be your joy if you should bring _____ unto me [Jesus]"

D&C 18:13

"How great is his [Jesus'] _____ in the soul that _____"

27

What's It Worth?

Advance Preparation

1. Cut out the family money found at the end of the lesson.
2. Collect several different items which family members would "buy" in Auction activity (for example, box of cookies, small toy, magazine, etc.). Put them in a sack or box so they can't be seen until auction time.
3. Personal scriptures and marking pencils.
4. Review the rules for the game Name That Price found in the chapter "Games for Many Occasions" and prepare the necessary materials.

Activity: Auction

1. Distribute the family money evenly among the members of the family.

2. Take one of the items out of the sack, hold it up, and tell the family you are going to sell it to the highest bidder. Ask someone to begin bidding for the item. The highest bidder pays with family money and receives the item.

3. Continue to auction the items until all have spent their money or all of the items are gone.

Ask family members who they think got the most for their money and who got the most valuable item. Then ask the family members what they think are some of the most valuable things we can gain in this life and why they are valuable. Discuss what makes something valuable. Point out that the things that are of most value are the things that last forever. As a family make a list of all the things you can think of that last forever and then mark and discuss Doctrine and Covenants 15:6.

Game: Name That Price

Play the game Name That Price (the rules are found in the chapter "Games for Many Occasions").

28

Joseph Gives His Life

Advance Preparation

1. Read rules for Danger game found in chapter "Games for Many Occasions."
2. Cut out the six large Danger (simplified) activity cards found at the end of this lesson.
3. Cut out the fifty-four Danger word cards found at the end of this lesson. Shuffle them and put them in an open container.
4. Paper and pencil to keep score.

Activity: Danger (simplified version)

1. Give each individual one (or more) of the six activity cards.
2. One player gives verbal clues to the rest of the family, without using the three forbidden words. Another family member then gives the clues on the next word. Give a sixty-second time limit. (See Danger game rules in the chapter "Games for Many Occasions" for further clarifications.)
3. When all six words have been guessed, ask the family if they can guess what event in Church history is discussed in this lesson. (Death of Joseph Smith.)

Story

Throughout history great men and women have given their lives for the gospel. The word *martyr* is used to describe someone who sacrifices his or her life for the sake of something precious like the gospel. The Prophet Joseph Smith and his brother Hyrum died as martyrs.

Joseph and Hyrum were unjustly arrested and placed in Carthage Jail. The governor of the state said that he would protect them, but he took his army and left the city.

Joseph knew that he was going to be killed and felt very sad. Besides his brother Hyrum, two Apostles were with him in the jail—John Taylor, who would become the third President of the Church, and Willard Richards.

John Taylor had a beautiful singing voice, so Joseph asked him to sing for them. He sang one of Joseph's favorite hymns, "A Poor Wayfaring Man of Grief." When he had finished, Joseph asked him to sing it again.

About this time a mob of men surrounded the jail and started to shoot their weapons through the windows and doors. They had painted their faces black so that no one would recognize them.

The four prisoners were in an upstairs room that had no lock on the door. There was no way that they could keep the mob out of the room. They tried holding the door shut, but the mob fired bullets through the door. Soon it burst open, and bullets showered the room. One of the bullets hit Hyrum in the head and killed him.

Brother Taylor stood by the side of the door and tried to knock down the guns with his walking stick as they were poked through the doorway. But the prisoners realized that this would not slow down the mob for long, and they felt that they would soon be dead.

Brother Taylor rushed to a window on the other side of the room that was fifteen or twenty feet above the ground. A bullet from the doorway struck the back of his leg. He was falling out of the window to a sure death when another bullet came through the window and struck his pocket watch, which was in his vest pocket near his left breast. This actually saved his life, as the force of the bullet threw him back into the room. After being shot two more times, he rolled under the bed, and was hit once again but remained alive.

As Joseph attempted to leap from the window, three bullets hit him. He fell through the window. By the time he hit the ground, Joseph was dead.

Someone in the mob yelled that Joseph had leaped through the window, at which the men at the door ran outside to see what was happening. This gave John Taylor and Willard Richards a brief opportunity to escape. Brother Richards dragged the wounded John Taylor into another room and covered him with an old mattress to try to conceal him. He then awaited the mob, expecting to be killed shortly. The mob, however, thinking other members of the Church were coming to fight, became frightened and ran away from the jail. It would take many months for Brother Taylor to recover from his wounds, but he and Brother Richards would live to be witnesses of the events of that day.

The Prophet Joseph was not the only Latter-day Saint to become a martyr for the Church. Many hundreds of Saints died as they followed the Church leaders across the mountains and into the Salt Lake Valley. Many people have been killed or have died while serving the Lord. Others have not died for the Church but have spent their lives in service to the Lord and to his church. It is as important to live for the Church as it is to die for it. All of us can show how deeply we value the gospel by doing the things God wants us to do.

Game: Danger

Play Danger, using the fifty-four word cards (the rules for the game are found in the chapter "Games for Many Occasions").

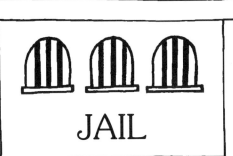

JAIL

Prison
Cell
Convict

MOB

Crowd
People
Many

INNOCENT

Blameless
Guilty
Faultless

SONG

Music
Voice
Tune

DEATH

End
Life
Funeral

WATCH

Clock
Time
Hand

REPENT	ANGEL	SCRIPTURES
Forgive Sins Jesus	Messenger Moroni Wings	Word Bible Books
TITHING	**PROPHET**	**CHASTITY**
Tenth Money Pay	President Seer Revelation	Virtue Purity Sex
CHARITY	**TEACHER**	**COVENANTS**
Love Christ Give	Class Students Church	Promises Contracts Deal
BLESSING	**SACRAMENT**	**ATONEMENT**
Priesthood Hands Sick	Ordinance Bread Water	Jesus Resurrected Forgive
FRIEND	**HAPPY**	**COURAGE**
Pal Buddy Do	Sad Joy Gospel	Fear Brave Pressure
SATAN	**PLATES**	**COURTESY**
Devil Lucifer Person	Gold Book Translate	Manners Nice Pleasant

BEEHIVES	FAITH	ANGER
Girls	Believe	Mad
Twelve	Testimony	Temper
Women	Hope	Upset

CONFESSION	PRIMARY	APOSTLE
Tell	Children	Twelve
Secret	Sunday	Jesus
Admit	Organization	Quorum

SERVICE	SPIRIT	SIN
Help	Body	Wrong
Share	Ghost	Bad
Wait	Spook	Commandments

COMPETITION	CONTENTION	CONFIRMATION
Sports	Arguing	Holy
Games	Fighting	Baptize
Win	Devil	Gift

PRIESTHOOD	PRAYER	BISHOP
Melchizedek	Kneel	Ward
Aaronic	Ask	Father
Authority	God	Leader

SCOUTS	WAGON	APPRECIATION
Camping	Pioneers	Gratitude
Eagle	Plains	Thankful
Boys	Covered	Positive

Danger Word Cards

THOUGHTS Brain Ideas Mind	**TESTIMONY** Know Faith Spirit	**TEMPTATION** Sin Wrong Entice
TEMPLE Marry Holy Baptisms	**TALENTS** Gifts Music Well	**SWEAR** Curse Name Promise
SUSTAIN Vote Accept Hands	**LUST** Love Desire Sex	**MODESTY** Dress Body Skin
MILLENNIUM Thousand Years Peace	**MORMON** Member Church Abridged	**OPPOSITION** Trials Problems Hardship
PATIENCE Tolerance Calm Wait	**PEACE** War Safety Fighting	**PERSECUTION** Abuse Harass Pick
PERSISTENCE Stick Keep Continue	**PONDERING** Think Meditate Reflect	**PRIDE** Humble Conceit Better

29

Forgive One Another
D & C 64:8–11

Advance Preparation

1. Pencil and paper for each family member.
2. Get a large stocking and place ten household items inside it such as a spoon, a small ball, a stapler, a small toy soldier, tweezers, an audio tape, a small ruler, a screwdriver, etc. Tie the end of the stocking.
3. Copies of the Doctrine and Covenants for each family member.
4. Study the rules for the game Hoops found in the chapter "Games for Many Occasions." Obtain a container for a basket and some masking tape and prepare them as described in the game rules for Hoops.

Activity: What's Inside?

1. Allow each family member two minutes to feel the contents of the stocking. During the two minutes, the person tries to identify and privately write down what he or she thinks the items are.

2. When everyone has had a turn, the contents are shown as each person checks the answer on his or her paper.

Scripture

The stocking activity demonstrates that it is difficult to judge what's inside something by how it looks or feels. This is especially true of people. We can see what people do, but we cannot see inside to understand *why* they do things or how they feel. Because of this, God has given us some very important counsel found in Doctrine and Covenants 64:8–11.

Have everyone turn to the scripture and discuss it. Some of the following ideas may be helpful to you:

1. In verse 8, what is the word that God uses to describe the act of not forgiving others? (*Evil.*)

2. What happened to the disciples who refused to forgive one another? (They were "afflicted and sorely chastened." This happens naturally, because unforgiveness breeds hate, anger, and revenge. These feelings drive away the Spirit of God and destroy our hearts and souls. No person who is holding a grudge or seeking revenge can ever be truly happy.)

3. Tell the family that you are going to tell a true story. Then they will be asked to decide what it has to do with forgiveness.

While picnicking in the desert with some friends, a teenage girl was bitten by a rattlesnake. Instead of immediately taking care of the bite and trying to get the poison out of her system, the girl and her friends chased after the snake. It took them fifteen minutes to find the snake and kill it, and by this time the poison had penetrated deeply into the girl's tissue

213

and blood. Because of her desire for revenge, she ended up having her leg amputated just below the knee. It was a high price to pay.

What does this story have to do with forgiving others? (The most deadly poison of all is the poison of unforgiveness. Other poisons damage the body, but unforgiveness can damage the soul. Just as in the story the girl should have immediately gotten the poison out of her system, when we are offended we need to *immediately* begin the process of forgiveness. The longer we wait, the harder it is and the more damage we suffer.)

4. Ask the family what they can do if they try to forgive someone but can't seem to do it. (God has promised us that if we do our best he will give us the strength to forgive others. Many people have testified of times when God has removed the bitterness and hate from their hearts and replaced those feelings with peace and forgiveness. Sometimes this happens quickly and sometimes it takes time. But if we do our best and ask the Lord to help, we can forgive all offenses.)

5. Have family members think privately if they are holding a grudge against someone. If they are, encourage them to ask God to help them forgive that person.

Game: Hoops

Play Hoops (the rules are found in the chapter "Games for Many Occasions"), using the questions from lessons 1 through 29 found in the chapter "Game Questions." The children's questions at the back of the book can also be used.

30

Brigham Young Becomes President

Advance Preparation

1. A clock with numbers, or a simple drawing of the face of a clock (one is provided at the end of the lesson).
2. Review instructions for Golfo game found in chapter "Games for Many Occasions," and prepare the materials. You will need sixteen paper cups, masking tape, putter, and golf ball or other small ball.
3. Cut out the Golfo game grids found at the end of this lesson.

Activity: Time for Magic

1. Tell the family you can do a magic trick. Tell them that if they choose a number on the clock while you are in another room, you can tell them which number they chose.
2. Leave the room and have the family choose one of the numbers on the clock.
3. When you come back in the room, tell them you are going to tap on the clock to get the answer. Ask them to silently count along with each tap, starting with the number they chose plus one. (For example, if they chose the number three, they would start counting quietly to themselves with the number four.) When they reach the number twenty, they must yell "Stop." Now tell them the correct number.

(Here's the trick: You also count the taps to yourself, *beginning with one.* Tap any place on the clock until the eighth tap. On the eighth tap, be sure to tap the number twelve. Then, with each tap, point to each number moving *counterclockwise* until the group tells you to stop. If no one has made a mistake, you will always stop at the number the family has chosen.)

Story

When we don't understand the principles that make things happen, we sometimes call these things magic or miracles. As in the clock trick above, once we understand the trick, we realize that it follows simple laws.

Because of the great power and knowledge of God, he performs many acts that we call miracles. One of God's most important miracles happened shortly after the death of Joseph Smith.

In general, the members of the Church were confused after the death of Joseph. Since he was the first President of the restored Church, they had never before had to seek a new leader. They didn't know how the next prophet would be selected.

To make things worse, most of the Twelve Apostles were away from Nauvoo on missions and were not able to help and direct the people. Brigham Young was President of the Quorum of the Twelve Apostles, and he knew that the Twelve Apostles held the priesthood keys for directing the Church. The problem was that he was in another state when he heard about Joseph's death.

Even though the Twelve Apostles had authority from God to guide the Church, several men tried to take over the leadership of the Church. One of these men was Sidney Rigdon, who tried to get the members to choose him as their leader before Brigham Young could return to Nauvoo.

However, Brigham Young returned in time, and a special conference was called to decide who would lead the Church. Sidney Rigdon spoke at the morning meeting. He was a great speaker and spoke for an hour and a half, but he could not convince the members of the Church that he was called by God to lead them.

Brigham Young spoke in the afternoon. Because God wanted everyone to know that Brigham Young should lead the Church, He performed a great miracle. As Brigham Young was speaking, it seemed to many present that he looked and sounded just like Joseph Smith. It was God's way of showing the people that Brigham Young should follow Joseph as the next leader of the Church. After witnessing this great miracle and feeling the Spirit of the Holy Ghost, all of the Church members present voted to sustain Brigham Young and the other members of the Quorum of the Twelve as the leaders of the Church.

God knows who he wants to lead his Church, and he prepares them so that they will be ready. He prepared Brigham Young, and he prepares his prophets today. When a prophet dies and a new one is chosen, we can be sure that he has been chosen and prepared by God.

Game: Golfo

Use any of the questions from lessons 1 through 30 to play Golfo (rules are found in the chapter "Games for Many Occasions"). Select the questions from the chapters "Game Questions" and "Children's Questions."

GOLF

1	16	14	3
15	2	6	10
9	7	5	4
13	8	12	11

GOLF

2	11	4	15
5	13	1	8
12	16	3	10
9	6	14	7

GOLF

4	7	10	14
9	12	3	11
6	1	8	16
2	15	13	5

GOLF

5	13	11	2
4	1	15	9
8	14	6	12
10	3	16	7

GOLF

7	15	3	11
10	5	9	4
2	16	12	14
1	13	6	8

GOLF

12	14	6	9
7	3	13	2
5	8	1	10
11	16	4	15

GOLF

11	15	1	4
2	14	9	12
7	3	13	16
5	11	6	10

GOLF

10	3	15	6
13	8	2	10
1	16	14	5
16	4	7	9

GOLF

16	4	3	12
8	13	7	15
11	9	14	5
2	6	10	1

31

Wait

Advance Preparation

1. Stopwatch or clock with a second hand.
2. Cut out the letter cards found at the end of this lesson.
3. Cut out the statement sheets found at the end of this lesson.

Activity

1. Divide the family into two teams.
2. Instruct the family that on the word *go* you are going to start measuring one minute by the clock. They should also try to measure one minute, but without a clock. When they think one minute is up they are to say "Stop." When the first team says "Stop," you look at the clock. If they are on the time within ten seconds either way, they receive two points. If they are within five seconds either way, they receive five points. If the guess was exactly right, they receive ten points. If they are more than ten seconds either way, they receive no points. The other team receives no points for the round. Only the first team to say "Stop" has a chance to receive points.
3. Do five rounds with a one-minute time limit, three rounds with a two-minute limit, and then two rounds with a three-minute limit. Score the points the same for each round.

Hint: While the time is running, talk to the family members and ask them questions. It will make it hard for them to count in their heads when they have to think about what you are saying.

Application

Ask what was difficult in this activity. One hard thing is to wait before saying "Stop." One of the hardest things for us to do when we pray to Heavenly Father is to wait. We have a hard time being quiet and waiting for Heavenly Father to talk to us. Ask the family how we could improve our prayers if we waited *before* praying; *during* prayer; *after* praying. (Before we pray, wait and think about what we should pray about and who we are praying to. During our prayer, stop and wait for thoughts, feelings, impressions, etc. After we pray, wait and think about the things we prayed for and how we felt. Waiting before, during, and after prayer gives Heavenly Father time to talk to us rather than leaving time only for our talk.) You may also want to discuss as a family the ways Heavenly Father talks to us when we pray.

Game

1. Divide the family into pairs and give each pair a statement sheet.
2. Put the lettercards face down on the floor or table.
3. Turn over the top letter card. For one minute each pair must write one answer to

each statement, and each answer must begin with the letter turned over. (For example, if the statement reads "Someone we should pray for," and the letter is *M,* a pair could write "Missionaries.")

4. At the end of the one minute, each pair shares what they have written down, statement by statement. A pair receives one point if none of the other pairs have written down the same answer. If any of the other pairs have the same word, neither pair receives any points for that answer.

5. Continue play until all of the letter cards have been turned over.

Statement	Round 1	Round 2	Round 3	Round 4
Something we should pray for	_____	_____	_____	_____
Someone we should pray for	_____	_____	_____	_____
Something we thank God for	_____	_____	_____	_____
A place we could pray	_____	_____	_____	_____
A prophet who prayed	_____	_____	_____	_____

Statement	Round 1	Round 2	Round 3	Round 4
Something we should pray for	_____	_____	_____	_____
Someone we should pray for	_____	_____	_____	_____
Something we thank God for	_____	_____	_____	_____
A place we could pray	_____	_____	_____	_____
A prophet who prayed	_____	_____	_____	_____

Statement	Round 1	Round 2	Round 3	Round 4
Something we should pray for	_____	_____	_____	_____
Someone we should pray for	_____	_____	_____	_____
Something we thank God for	_____	_____	_____	_____
A place we could pray	_____	_____	_____	_____
A prophet who prayed	_____	_____	_____	_____

S

M

T

P

32

Word of Wisdom
D & C 89

Advance Preparation

1. Cut out the six picture matches found at the end of this lesson.
2. Marking pencil and a copy of the Doctrine and Covenants for each family member.
3. Review the game Seek and Destroy found in the chapter "Games for Many Occasions." The materials are found at the end of this lesson. Cut out the master sheet and enough grid sheets for each family member. (Only you should see the master sheet.)

Activity: Story and Picture Match

1. Give the following background about the Word of Wisdom:

The first School of the Prophets was held upstairs over the Prophet Joseph's kitchen. These meetings were held in a very small room that was not larger than eleven feet by fourteen feet.

Some church members traveled hundreds of miles to attend these meetings and be instructed by the Prophet. When they assembled together, the first thing they did was light their pipes and, while smoking, talk about the great things of the kingdom. Many of them would chew tobacco and spit the juice on the floor.

Often when the Prophet entered the room to give them instructions he would find himself in a cloud of tobacco smoke. This, and comments from his wife about the filthiness of the room, caused the Prophet to think about the situation. When he prayed and asked the Lord about it, he received the revelation known as the Word of Wisdom, which is now section 89 of the Doctrine and Covenants. (See Brigham Young's comments in *Journal of Discourses* 12:158.)

2. Pass out a copy of the Picture Match to each family member and have them respond to the eight questions. Pair younger children with older family members who can read the questions for them.

Scriptures: The Importance of the Body

In order to better understand the importance of the Word of Wisdom, we need to understand how vital our physical bodies are. The following scriptures teach us the importance of our bodies. Have family members look up the following scriptures and see if they can figure out what the scriptures are teaching about our bodies. Mark each scripture before moving on.

1. *D&C 130:22*—God has a body of flesh and bone. We came here to become like God, which includes receiving a physical body.
2. *D&C 93:33-34*—The body is made of elements. The spirit and body joined forever can have a fulness of joy. Without a physical body, we could never have a fulness of joy.

227

3. *D&C 93:35*—Our bodies are temples, and we should treat them with reverence. Ask family members if they would swear or tell dirty stories or fight or watch bad movies in the temple. If not, they should not allow these things in their body-temples.

4. *Alma 34:36*—The Spirit of God does not dwell in unholy temples.

5. *D&C 88:15*—The spirit and the body are the soul of man.

6. *D&C 138:17*—Once the spirit and the body reunite in the resurrection, they will never separate again.

7. *D&C 138:50*—Separation of body and spirit is a kind of bondage.

8. *Alma 11:43-45*—In the resurrection we receive immortal bodies that are perfectly formed.

Scripture Activity: Name That Verse

The Word of Wisdom teaches us how to keep our physical temples clean and pure so the Spirit of the Lord can be with us. Use the following activity to help the family become better acquainted with the Word of Wisdom:

Divide the family into groups and have them turn to section 89 in the Doctrine and Covenants. Tell them you will read a question. They should quickly find the verse that answers the question and yell out the number of the verse. The team that finds the correct verse first reads the verse aloud to the rest of the family. Read the first question and follow this procedure until all of the questions have been answered. You may want to discuss some of the verses as you read them.

1. What is tobacco supposed to be used for? (Verse 8. Sick cattle.)

2. What reason does God give for warning and forewarning us by giving us the Word of Wisdom? (Verse 4. The evils and designs which exist in the hearts of conspiring men. Such men, knowing that the things they make and sell destroy our health and even kill many people, meet together to plan how they can get more people to use their products so they can make more money.)

3. Name one of the promises of the Word of Wisdom. (Verses 18-21. Most of these promises are spiritual in nature. Discuss some spiritual meanings for "walk and not faint" and "run and not be weary." [For example, receiving the power to overcome obstacles; remaining true to the faith.] Of course there are great physical blessings that come automatically from living the Word of Wisdom.)

4. What three verses talk about alcoholic beverages or strong drinks? (Verses 5-7.)

5. What grain does God say can be made into a mild drink? (Verse 17. Barley.)

6. The words *wholesome, prudence* (which means caution and wisdom), and *thanksgiving* are sometimes called the spirit of the Word of Wisdom. These qualities help us judge what we should eat and drink. In which two verses are these three words found? (Verses 10-11. Have the family circle these three words and discuss what each one means.)

7. What has God ordained or chosen to be the staff of life? (Verse 14. Grains.)

8. In which city was the Word of Wisdom received? (Section heading or verse 1. Kirtland.)

9. Where does it say that the Word of Wisdom is "adapted to the capacity of . . . the weakest of all saints"? (Verse 3. This suggests that the Word of Wisdom is a minimum requirement for the Saints. This may be why it is one of the requirements for obtaining a temple recommend and for advancement in the priesthood.)

10. Where does it say that hot drinks are not for the body or belly? (Verse 9. Some people have sometimes misinterpreted what is meant by hot drinks and have thought that it had to do with the temperature of beverages that we drink. This would mean that hot chocolate is against the Word of Wisdom but iced tea is not. This question is resolved by a reported statement from Joseph Smith that indicates the Lord meant *tea and coffee* when

he said "hot drinks" [*see* Joel H. Johnson, *Voice from the Mountains* (Salt Lake City: Juvenile Instructor Office, 1881), p. 12].)

Conclusion

Now that the activity is over, the family may have some questions, or you may desire to clarify or discuss some other aspects of the Word of Wisdom. Tea, coffee, alcoholic beverages, and tobacco are the four main "don'ts" of the Word of Wisdom. Church leaders have strongly counselled us against using some other things, such as drugs not needed for medication.

The Word of Wisdom also gives us three governing principles concerning foods and beverages: (1) *Wholesomeness*—"Are they good for us?" (2) *Prudence*—"Would it be wise to use them?" (3) *Thanksgiving*—"Do we appreciate the good things that God has given us?" These three important questions can help us keep our bodies clean.

Game: Seek and Destroy

The rules for Seek and Destroy are found in the chapter "Games for Many Occasions."

Tell the family that they are going to seek out and destroy things that are spiritually harmful to us. Also tell them that they will be penalized if they try to destroy something that is good for us.

Use any of the questions from lessons 1 through 32 (found in the chapter "Game Questions") to play the game. The children's questions at the back of the book may also be used.

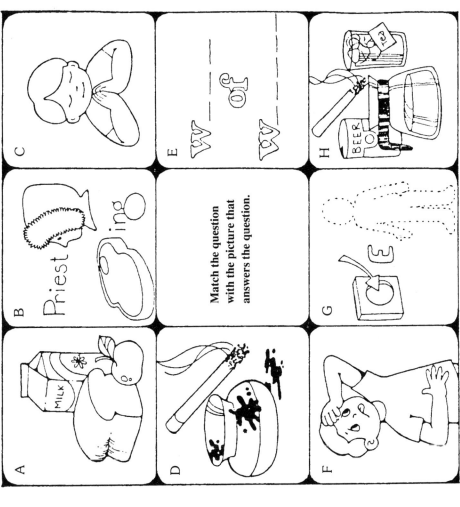

A   B Priest___ing   C

D   **Match the question with the picture that answers the question.**   E   w ___ of ___ w

F   G   H BEER

1. What kind of meeting did Joseph walk into?
2. What were the men doing in the meeting?
3. How did Joseph feel about the smoking and spitting?
4. When Joseph left the dirty room, what did he do?
5. What do we call the instructions that Joseph received?
6. What are the four things that the Word of Wisdom tells us not to use?
7. What are some foods that are good for us?
8. Who will be with us if we keep our bodies clean?

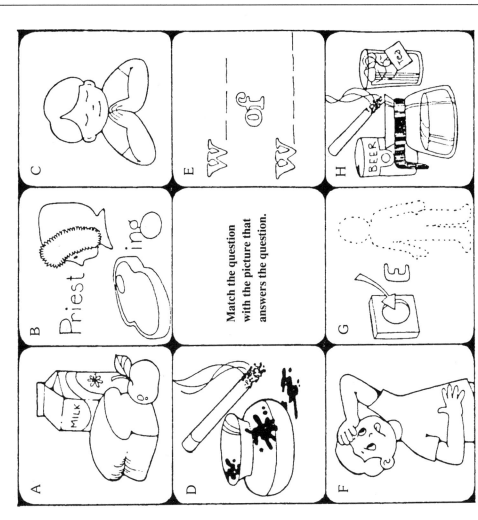

A   B Priest___ing   C

D   **Match the question with the picture that answers the question.**   E   w ___ of ___ w

F   G   H BEER

1. What kind of meeting did Joseph walk into?
2. What were the men doing in the meeting?
3. How did Joseph feel about the smoking and spitting?
4. When Joseph left the dirty room, what did he do?
5. What do we call the instructions that Joseph received?
6. What are the four things that the Word of Wisdom tells us not to use?
7. What are some foods that are good for us?
8. Who will be with us if we keep our bodies clean?

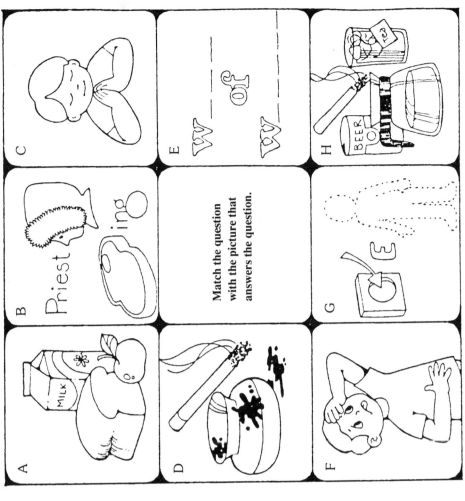

Match the question with the picture that answers the question.

1. What kind of meeting did Joseph walk into?
2. What were the men doing in the meeting?
3. How did Joseph feel about the smoking and spitting?
4. When Joseph left the dirty room, what did he do?
5. What do we call the instructions that Joseph received?
6. What are the four things that the Word of Wisdom tells us not to use?
7. What are some foods that are good for us?
8. Who will be with us if we keep our bodies clean?

Match the question with the picture that answers the question.

1. What kind of meeting did Joseph walk into?
2. What were the men doing in the meeting?
3. How did Joseph feel about the smoking and spitting?
4. When Joseph left the dirty room, what did he do?
5. What do we call the instructions that Joseph received?
6. What are the four things that the Word of Wisdom tells us not to use?
7. What are some foods that are good for us?
8. Who will be with us if we keep our bodies clean?

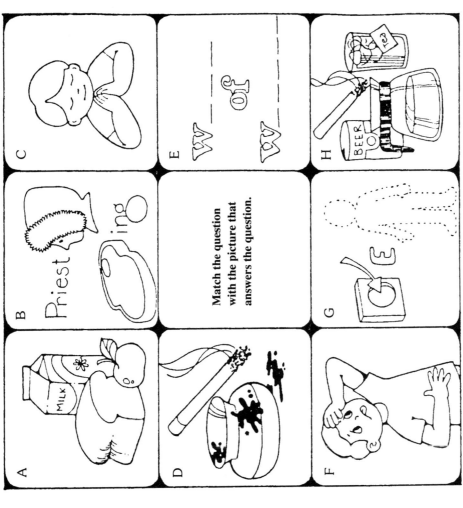

Match the question with the picture that answers the question.

1. What kind of meeting did Joseph walk into?
2. What were the men doing in the meeting?
3. How did Joseph feel about the smoking and spitting?
4. When Joseph left the dirty room, what did he do?
5. What do we call the instructions that Joseph received?
6. What are the four things that the Word of Wisdom tells us not to use?
7. What are some foods that are good for us?
8. Who will be with us if we keep our bodies clean?

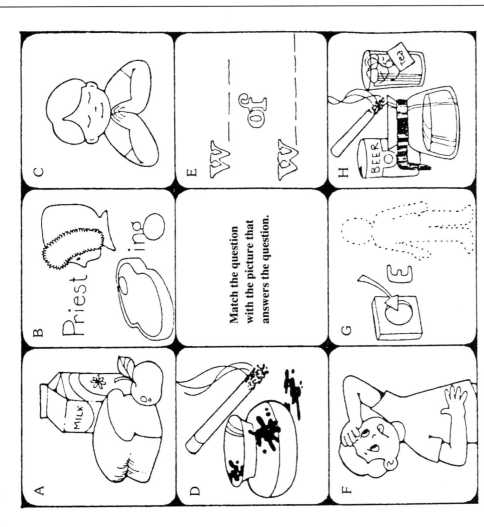

Match the question with the picture that answers the question.

1. What kind of meeting did Joseph walk into?
2. What were the men doing in the meeting?
3. How did Joseph feel about the smoking and spitting?
4. When Joseph left the dirty room, what did he do?
5. What do we call the instructions that Joseph received?
6. What are the four things that the Word of Wisdom tells us not to use?
7. What are some foods that are good for us?
8. Who will be with us if we keep our bodies clean?

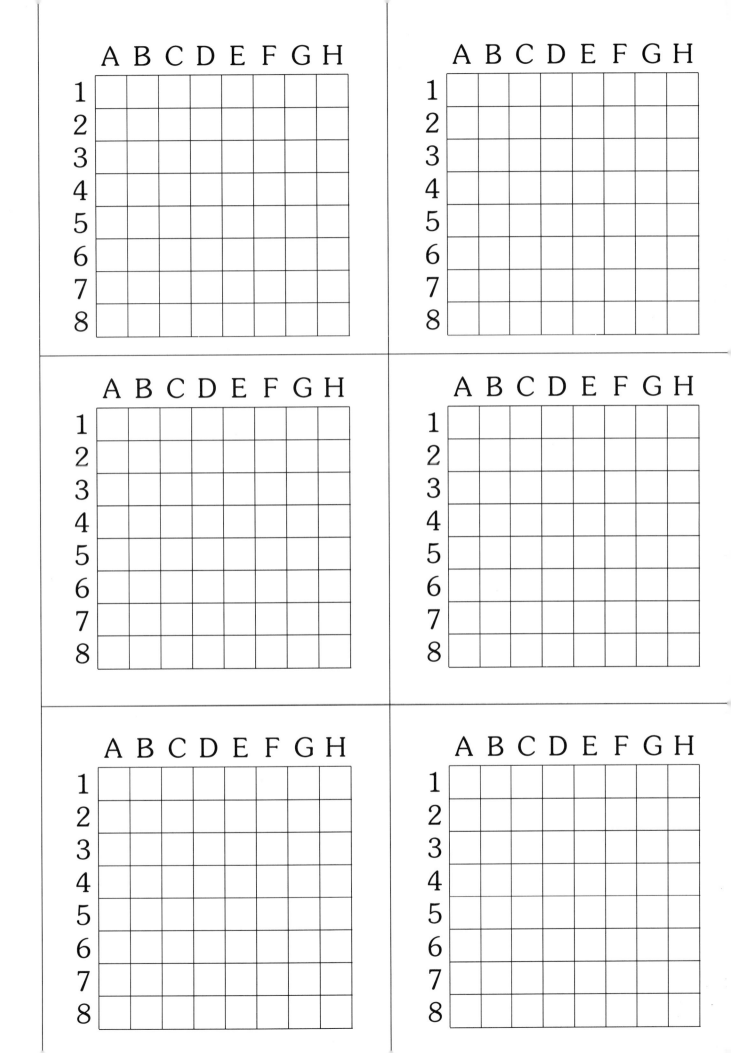

	A	B	C	D	E	F	G	H
1								
2								
3								
4								
5								
6								
7								
8								

	A	B	C	D	E	F	G	H
1								
2								
3								
4								
5								
6								
7								
8								

Master Sheet

	A	B	C	D	E	F	G	H
1				S	G	U	R	D
2	L	I	E				TITHING	
3				KIND	L		A	
4		L		I			N	
5		A	V	HONESTY			G	
6	PRAYER	E					E	
7	D	T					R	
8		S						

33

Crossing the Plains Activity

Introduction

This activity is based on actual experiences of the early Mormon pioneers. The original pioneer company took about fifteen weeks to travel from Winter Quarters to the Salt Lake Valley. In the game, each campsite represents one week of that journey. The three options at each campsite are based on the pioneers' actual experiences. As your family plays the game, they will become familiar with many different pioneer experiences.

Objective

The objective of the activity is to become the "best pioneer" by earning the most points by the time all of the players reach the Salt Lake Valley.

Instructions for Playing

1. Cut out the twelve Crossing the Plains squares found at the end of this lesson, and place them in an open container. Cut out the supply record sheets that can also be found at the end of this lesson.

2. Give each player a supply record and a pencil. Have them write the numerals from 1 to 15 on the back of their supply records. Young children can be teamed with older family members.

3. Tell the family members to pretend to be pioneers preparing to leave Winter Quarters. Each one starts out with a wagon, a team of oxen, enough food to cross the plains, and $170 in cash.

4. Have them look at their supply record sheets. Each person should choose from this list any supplies he wants to purchase before leaving Winter Quarters. Have them fill in the first column ("Original Purchases") by following these directions:

   (a) Write down the quantity of any item you decide to purchase. (For example, if you decide you want to take two boxes of ammunition with you, write 2 on the line next to "Box of ammunition.")

   (b) Note the cost of your purchases and subtract them from your cash ($170 when you start).

   (c) You may decide to keep some cash. If you do, enter that amount in the box next to "Cash."

5. Explain to the family members that the rest of the activity will be a paper-and-pencil replay of a pioneer trek. There will be fifteen "campsites." At each one they will receive some information. You will read that information, then allow a few moments so that each person can write down an A, B, or C next to the appropriate campsite number on the back side of the supply record. You will then read the consequences of each of those choices and give them time to record any losses or gains on their supply record sheets.

6. If a player chooses an option that has an asterisk (*) next to it, he follows the

241

instructions from that option, but he also draws a Crossing the Plains square and follows the directions given there.

7. Each player should keep a running record of supplies in the "Losses and Gains" columns. For any change, enter the number of *items the player still has.* (For instance, if a player had purchased two boxes of ammunition and now has to give one of them to another player, he would write the number *1* in the first empty box on the ammunition line under "Losses and Gains." This is because he has only one box of ammunition left. If a player had purchased two snakebite kits and now receives another one, he would write the number *3* in the first empty box on the snakebite kit line because he now has three snakebite kits.)

To Begin Play

1. Read the heading for Campsite 1. Each player then selects the letter *A, B,* or *C* and records the choice next to the number *1* written on the back of the supply record.

2. Next, read the options at this campsite so that players can hear the results of their choices. They should record their gains or losses on their supply records accordingly. (Note: If a player chooses something that cannot be done with his supplies, tell him to ignore it and make no changes at that campsite. Also, when an option requires that an unspecified supply item be given, the one *giving* the item decides what it will be. When an option indicates that a player receives or gives an item, other players are not involved unless specific mention is made in the directions.)

3. When every player has completed his turn at Campsite 1, read the introductory information for Campsite 2. Continue as explained.

4. Instructions for scoring are found at the end of the activity.

Campsite 1

The Elkhorn River is one of the first obstacles that you face. It is a difficult crossing, and all of the wagons have to be ferried across on a raft.
  A. If you have an ax and rope, you help build cottonwood rafts. If you do not have an ax and rope, someone else has to help you, and you subtract one item of your choice as payment.
  B. Several men need their horses shod. If you have blacksmith tools, collect $5 either in cash or supplies from each player who does not have blacksmith tools.
  C. Brigham Young asks the camp not to hunt or fish on Sundays and you decide to take his counsel. Add a $10 item of your choice as a reward.

Campsite 2

You make good time as you cross the level Nebraska prairie. You decide to follow the north bank of the Platte River.
  A. You have a severe toothache and finally pay Brother Luke Johnson $5 to pull your tooth. Subtract $5 or a supply item of your choice.
* B. Two hundred Pawnee Indians meet the wagon train, and you are worried. But they turn out to be friendly and you trade one item of your choice for two blankets.
  C. You catch two hundred fish in just a few hours. Gain one week's supply of food if you have fishing gear.

Campsite 3

You have a real struggle crossing the Loup Fork because of the quicksand. But once you are across, you head cross-country toward the Platte River. Along the Platte there are very few trees, so you decide to use buffalo chips for fuel.

  *A. While you are on guard you hear a rustling noise in the grass and scare away six Indians. Receive $5 in cash or a supply item from each player.

   B. Since you are one of the first wagons to cross the river, you have to totally unload your wagon to keep from bogging down in the quicksand. You lose your plow in the process.

   C. While waiting to cross the river, one of your horses falls into a ravine and chokes on the rope around his neck. Lose one horse.

Campsite 4

Indians start prairie fires along the route. Most of the grass burns; the rest has been eaten away by buffalo. Your oxen are left with little to eat.

  *A. Brigham Young chooses you as a scout to ride ahead and find areas of unburned grass. Gain a rifle and a box of ammunition if you have a horse.

   B. While returning to camp you sight two antelope and shoot them both. Gain one week's supply of food if you have a rifle and ammunition.

   C. You quickly write a letter, and it is taken back to your family in Winter Quarters by a French trader. This costs you $5 in cash or a supply item.

Campsite 5

Buffalo surround your wagons, and there are buffalo as far as you can see. Your livestock suffer because the buffalo have eaten all of the grass.

   A. You eat bad buffalo meat, which makes you sick. Lose one item of your choice.

   B. You kill two wolves and sell caps made out of their fur. Collect $5 in cash or a supply item from each player if you have a rifle and ammunition.

   C. You wash your socks, towel, handkerchief, and yourself in the freezing water of the Platte River and catch a cold. Lose one blanket unless you have cayenne pepper to help you feel better.

Campsite 6

The odometer is attached to a wagon. It keeps track of how many times the wagon wheel turns around, so you can figure how many miles you travel each day. This will help in making accurate maps for future pioneers.

   A. While crossing Rattlesnake Creek, you are bitten by a rattler. Give $20 dollars in cash or supplies for a snakebite kit, unless you already have one.

   B. As a rattlesnake attacks Thomas Woolsey, you shoot the head off the snake. If you have a rifle and ammunition, collect one more rifle and another box of ammunition for being such a good shot.

  *C. Your wagon becomes bogged down in rolling sand hills, and you throw out one item in order to make pulling the wagon easier for your oxen.

Campsite 7

You are excited when you reach Chimney Rock because you know you are almost halfway to the Salt Lake Valley. Chimney Rock is about 260 feet high and can be seen more than forty miles away.

A. The temperature drops sharply, and sixteen horses freeze to death. If you don't have at least two blankets to wrap your horse in, lose one horse.

* B. Your team runs away with your wagon, and a wheel is broken. If you do not have a wheel repair kit, buy one for $10 from a player who has one. If you do not have cash, you may choose any one of your supply items as payment.

C. Porter Rockwell shoots two antelope and shares the meat with you. Gain one week's supply of food.

Campsite 8

You reach Fort Laramie and ferry the wagons across the Platte River. You change to the south bank of the river, which puts you on the Oregon Trail.

* A. You take part in a special prayer meeting with Brigham Young and other Church leaders. Add an item of your choice.

B. You help Luke Johnson do some doctoring at Fort Laramie and receive $20 in cash, supplies, or a combination of both.

C. You pick several prickly pears, peel the skins away, and find that they are delicious. Gain one week's supply of food.

Campsite 9

As you follow the Oregon Trail, you meet wagon trains from Missouri. You continually leap-frog each other in order to obtain the best campsites.

A. On a sharp turn at the bottom of a hill, your wagon turns over. If you do not have a rope and pulley, give an item of your choice to a player who does.

B. Members of the wagon train take a relaxing bath and wash their clothes in a warm spring known as Emigrants Laundry. They decide to make the day complete by relaxing with a good glass of milk. Each player who does not have a milk cow gives you an item of their choice if you own a milk cow.

C. Rain and hail destroy part of your wagon cover. You have to trade a set of fishing gear for the materials needed to repair it. Lose one set of fishing gear.

Campsite 10

You reach the North Platte River, one hundred yards wide, and swollen by spring runoff. You have the longest delay of the entire trek while you make rafts.

A. You help save a Missourian who tries to swim across the river. Not only do you win his friendship, but he gives you a sack of seeds to show his gratitude.

B. All around the campsite the ground seems to be alive with large crickets. Some of them get into your seeds. Lose one sack of seeds.

* C. While crossing the river, you forget to take the rope off one of your horses. The rope tangles up in his legs and he drowns. Lose one horse.

Campsite 11

Once across the North Platte, you move southwest to the Sweetwater River. This takes you three days through a barren wasteland.

A. You climb Independence Rock and see hundreds of names painted on the rock. During your climb you pick wild strawberries and gooseberries. Gain one week's supply of food.

* B. You see the mountains in the distance and notice that they are covered with snow. You buy or trade something of your choice for two extra blankets.
  C. While crossing a small brook, your wagon axle breaks. You have to use your rope to lash a piece of wood against the axle. Lose one rope. If you do not have a rope, a player of your choice takes one of your items (his choice) and loses his rope.

Campsite 12

You reach the Sweetwater River and enter South Pass. While in the pass, you cross the Continental Divide, where the rivers begin to flow west instead of east.
  A. You cross the Continental Divide on the date Joseph and Hyrum Smith were killed three years ago. You spend the rest of the day in meditation. The Lord blesses you, and your equipment lasts longer. Take a $10 supply item of your choice.
  B. A mysterious fever moves through the company. One supply item is lost while you are sick.
  C. The camp is running short on water, and you can sell milk if you have a milk cow. Collect $5 in cash or supplies from each player who doesn't own a milk cow.

Campsite 13

After crossing the Green River, you rest for a few days. You then head south through dry country until you find water. You finally reach Fort Bridger, where you have an opportunity to replenish your supplies.
  A. If you wish to, and have cash, you may spend up to $20 on supplies.
* B. If you wish to, and have cash, you may spend up to $40 on supplies.
  C. If you wish to, and have cash, you may spend up to $60 on supplies.

Campsite 14

You are having difficulty improving the trail. Brigham Young comes down with mountain fever, and an advance party is chosen to go on ahead.
* A. The company is split, and you are put in the advance guard. You receive the honor of being one of the first to enter the Salt Lake Valley. If you have a horse, you get to the valley early and start to plant crops. Gain one week's supply of food if you have a horse.
  B. While exploring, you discover oil bubbling out of the ground. It has ruined the drinking water, but you share some of it with others so they can oil their rifles and boots. Those players with rifles give you $5 in money or a supply item of their choice.
  C. You use your ax to clear the way through the thick brush and trees in Echo Canyon. Lose one item of your choice if you do not have an ax.

Campsite 15

You follow the route of the Donner Party and leave Echo Canyon. Thirty-six miles of rugged mountains lie between you and the Salt Lake Valley.
  A. The same stream has to be recrossed thirteen times. You lose one of your sacks of seeds.
  B. Your oxen are too tired to pull your wagon up Little Mountain. If you have a horse and rope, you make it to the top. If you do not have one or both of these items, you buy them at double their cost from a player of your choice who has them. The

horse now costs $100, and the rope now costs $10. You can pay for them in cash or with supply items.

* C. Your wagon wheels collapse on a steep hill. If you do not have a wheel repair kit, pay a player of your choice $20 or its equivalent in supplies for repairs.

Finish: Salt Lake Valley

Now that you have reached the Salt Lake Valley, you can begin to plow and plant. If you do not have a plow and seeds, it will be a very long, hungry winter, so these are now your most valuable supplies.

Add up your points to see which player was the best pioneer.

Scoring

Score one point for each dollar value. (Example: A horse cost $50 so it is worth 50 points.) However, plows are worth 100 points each and bags of seeds are worth 20 points each (double their dollar value).

Players with the most points are the best pioneers.

Take one item of your choice from the person on your left.	Gain one milk cow.	Give one item of your choice to the supply wagon.
Give one item of your choice to a person of your choice.	Gain one plow.	Take one item of your choice from a person of your choice.
Take one item of your choice from the person on your right.	Lose one plow.	Lose one milk cow.
Take one item of your choice from the supply wagon.	Gain one sack of seeds.	Lose one sack of seeds.

Supply Record

	Original Purchases	*Losses and Gains								Total Points
Set of fishing gear $5										
Rope $5										
Canister of cayenne pepper $5										
Blanket $5										
Snakebite kit $10										
Dog $10										
Box of ammunition $10										
Sack of seeds $10										
Ax $10										
Wheel repair kit $15										
Set of pulleys $20										
Set of blacksmith tools $20										
Rifle $30										
Milk Cow $40										
Horse $50										
Plow $50										
Cash										
Week's supply of food $10										

Score

Supply Record

	Original Purchases	*Losses and Gains								Total Points
Set of fishing gear $5										
Rope $5										
Canister of cayenne pepper $5										
Blanket $5										
Snakebite kit $10										
Dog $10										
Box of ammunition $10										
Sack of seeds $10										
Ax $10										
Wheel repair kit $15										
Set of pulleys $20										
Set of blacksmith tools $20										
Rifle $30										
Milk Cow $40										
Horse $50										
Plow $50										
Cash										
Week's supply of food $10										

Score

Supply Record

	Original Purchases	*Losses and Gains								Total Points
Set of fishing gear $5										
Rope $5										
Canister of cayenne pepper $5										
Blanket $5										
Snakebite kit $10										
Dog $10										
Box of ammunition $10										
Sack of seeds $10										
Ax $10										
Wheel repair kit $15										
Set of pulleys $20										
Set of blacksmith tools $20										
Rifle $30										
Milk Cow $40										
Horse $50										
Plow $50										
Cash										
Week's supply of food $10										

Score

Supply Record

	Original Purchases	*Losses and Gains								Total Points
Set of fishing gear $5										
Rope $5										
Canister of cayenne pepper $5										
Blanket $5										
Snakebite kit $10										
Dog $10										
Box of ammunition $10										
Sack of seeds $10										
Ax $10										
Wheel repair kit $15										
Set of pulleys $20										
Set of blacksmith tools $20										
Rifle $30										
Milk Cow $40										
Horse $50										
Plow $50										
Cash										
Week's supply of food $10										

Score

Supply Record

Item	Original Purchases	*Losses and Gains							Total Points
Set of fishing gear $5									
Rope $5									
Canister of cayenne pepper $5									
Blanket $5									
Snakebite kit $10									
Dog $10									
Box of ammunition $10									
Sack of seeds $10									
Ax $10									
Wheel repair kit $15									
Set of pulleys $20									
Set of blacksmith tools $20									
Rifle $30									
Milk Cow $40									
Horse $50									
Plow $50									
Cash									
Week's supply of food $10									

Score

Supply Record

Item	Original Purchases	*Losses and Gains							Total Points
Set of fishing gear $5									
Rope $5									
Canister of cayenne pepper $5									
Blanket $5									
Snakebite kit $10									
Dog $10									
Box of ammunition $10									
Sack of seeds $10									
Ax $10									
Wheel repair kit $15									
Set of pulleys $20									
Set of blacksmith tools $20									
Rifle $30									
Milk Cow $40									
Horse $50									
Plow $50									
Cash									
Week's supply of food $10									

Score

Supply Record

	Original Purchases	*Losses and Gains							Total Points
Set of fishing gear $5									
Rope $5									
Canister of cayenne pepper $5									
Blanket $5									
Snakebite kit $10									
Dog $10									
Box of ammunition $10									
Sack of seeds $10									
Ax $10									
Wheel repair kit $15									
Set of pulleys $20									
Set of blacksmith tools $20									
Rifle $30									
Milk Cow $40									
Horse $50									
Plow $50									
Cash									
Week's supply of food $10									

Score

Supply Record

	Original Purchases	*Losses and Gains							Total Points
Set of fishing gear $5									
Rope $5									
Canister of cayenne pepper $5									
Blanket $5									
Snakebite kit $10									
Dog $10									
Box of ammunition $10									
Sack of seeds $10									
Ax $10									
Wheel repair kit $15									
Set of pulleys $20									
Set of blacksmith tools $20									
Rifle $30									
Milk Cow $40									
Horse $50									
Plow $50									
Cash									
Week's supply of food $10									

Score

Resources

Key Scripture Ideas

Ten key scriptures are introduced in the lessons. These scriptures can be reviewed over and over again by using the following activities and games. Some of the activities and games are included in the lessons. This section also describes other activities and games that you may do with your family anytime. If you don't like or understand an activity or game that is suggested in one of the lessons, choose another one that sounds more fun to you.

The activities and games below are listed in alphabetical order. For many of these you'll want to have on hand the three sets of Key Scripture cards from lesson 5.

Remember that you may include younger children by letting them be partners with older members of the family.

All or Nothing

1. Prepare a list of clues that will direct players to the key scriptures. You can use the Key Scripture statement cards for this purpose, or you may want to create some clues of your own.

2. Give each player a copy of the scriptures.

3. Divide the family into two teams. Tell them you will be giving them a clue and they should each find the correct key scripture in their books. Each player should raise his hand when he has found it. A team wins when *all* of its members find the scripture. Team members can help each other, if desired.

4. Start by reading a clue and letting the teams find the scripture. When they've finished, read the correct answer.

5. Continue by reading a new clue and letting the teams search.

6. If you wish to keep score, give one point in each round or give bonus points for more difficult clues.

(This game is used in lesson 13.)

Beat the Leader

1. Get a set of the Key Scripture cards used in lesson 5 (any of the three sets) and place them face down.

2. Give each family member a copy of the scriptures.

3. Choose one family member to be the scripture leader.

4. The scripture leader turns over the top card and each member of the family (including the scripture leader) looks for the matching scripture. Each family member who finds it before the scripture leader receives one point. The scripture leader receives one point for each family member he or she beats.

5. Choose a new scripture leader and continue until each family member has taken one turn as the scripture leader. The winner is the person with the most points.

6. You may want to give younger children a head start. This could be done by having

everyone else count to ten or twenty before starting.

(This game is used in lesson 9.)

Bowling

1. Prepare ten clues which will direct players to the key scriptures. You can use the Key Scripture statement cards for this purpose, or you may want to make up some clues of your own.

2. Give each family member a copy of the scriptures and a sheet which contains several lines for bowling scores (see example).

1	2	3	4	5	6	7	8	9	10
4 / 8	7 / 15	3 / 18	5 / 23						

3. Choose one family member to be the scripture leader. He gives the first scripture clue and begins to count backwards from ten ("10-9-8-7-6-5-4-3-2-1-gutter").

4. As soon as the clue is given, everyone begins to look for the scripture. The number spoken just before they find the scripture is the number they score for that particular frame.

5. Have the family members mark their sheets in the first frame (see example). Note that the scoring is not quite the same as in bowling. Score only once in each frame.

6. Have the scripture leader give another clue and count for each frame.

7. As the family learns the scriptures better, the count can be given faster. You can bowl as many frames and games as you desire.

Concentration

1. Get the Key Scripture cards from lesson 5. Any two of the three sets can be used. The Key Scripture picture cards and Key Scripture reference cards are used as examples in the following rules.

2. Shuffle the Key Scripture picture cards and scatter them face down in the center of the table or floor so that none of the cards are on top of each other.

3. Do the same thing with the Key Scripture reference cards, but in an area slightly separated from the first set.

4. The first player begins by turning over a Key Scripture picture card and a Key Scripture reference card. If they match, the player keeps them. If they do not match, they are placed face down again. Either way, it is now the next player's turn.

5. Each player takes a turn trying to find a matching pair of cards.

6. Play ends when all of the cards have been matched and removed from the table or floor. The player with the most cards is the winner.

I've Got a Question

1. Get the Key Scripture reference cards (from lesson 5) and put them in a bowl.

2. Divide the family into pairs and give each pair a sheet of paper and a pencil or pen. (If your family is small, you could play this game as individuals.)

3. Draw one card from the bowl and show it to all players.

4. On the word *go,* each pair has three minutes to write as many questions as they can that can be answered using the key scripture.

5. At the end of the three minutes each pair reads their questions and tells how the scripture answers it. They receive one point for each question and a bonus point for each question they had that none of the other pairs had.

6. Play continues until all of the Key Scripture reference cards have been drawn from the bowl.

(This game is played in lesson 21.)

The More the Merrier

1. Prepare clues that will direct the players to the key scriptures. Use the Key Scripture statement cards for this purpose, or make up some clues of your own.

2. Divide the family into two teams.

3. Working with one team, give a scripture clue to one member of the team. If he responds with the correct scriptural reference, give another scripture clue to the next member of the team. This continues until one of the team members gives an incorrect answer.

4. Do the same thing with the other team. The second team has to get at least as many correct answers as the first team in order to stay in the game. If the second team gets more, the first team will then have to match their score in order to stay in the game.

5. Play switches back and forth until one team gets a lower score than the other one. The team who achieved the higher score is the winner.

6. If you want to play again, try mixing the teams differently.

Read All About It!

1. Get the Key Scripture reference cards (from lesson 5) and put them in a bowl.

2. Divide the family into pairs and give paper and pencil to each pair. (If your family is small, you could play this game as individuals.)

3. Have each family member in turn draw from the bowl until all of the cards are gone.

4. Have each pair write on a piece of paper a newspaper headline for each scripture they have drawn.

5. Have the pairs take turns reading one of their headlines. The rest of the pairs have thirty seconds to turn to the scripture. Each pair that finds the correct scripture within the time limit earns one point.

Scripture Golf

1. The object of the game is to locate scriptures quickly. Family members who can do it quickly will have a lower score than those who take more time.

2. Draw an imaginary golf score card on a piece of paper and make copies for each family member. It should list nine holes along with as many games as desired. It might look something like this:

	Game 1	Game 2	Game 3	Game 4
1 (par 4)	____	____	____	____
2 (par 3)	____	____	____	____
3 (par 5)	____	____	____	____
4 (par 3)	____	____	____	____
5 (par 4)	____	____	____	____
etc.				

3. Choose a scripture leader.

4. The scripture leader gives a scripture clue that will direct players to one of the ten key scriptures (use the Key Scripture statement cards for this purpose, or make up your own clues), and then the scripture leader begins to count slowly from one to seven. The higher the par, the harder the hole, so the scripture leader will count faster on the par 5 holes than on the par 4 ones and faster on the par 4 holes than on the par 3 holes.

5. As soon as the clue is given, players begin to search for the scripture in their books. The number they hear right after they find the scripture is the score they receive on that hole. If they are unable to find the correct scripture or to find it by the count of seven, they score an eight.

6. Each person records his or her score in the appropriate spot and the game continues with the next scripture clue. (Several games may be scored on one score card, so the card can be saved and used again without wasting time and paper.)

7. When nine holes have been played (nine scriptures found), the person with the lowest score is the winner. If the game ends in a tie, then you could have a sudden-death playoff. The winners would play three additional holes. The person to find the scripture the fastest on each hole wins that hole. The final winner is the person to win two out of the three holes.

Scripture March

1. Get a copy of the scriptures for each member of the family. Place them at intervals around a table.

2. Select the same number of Key Scripture picture cards or Key Scripture statement cards (from lesson 5) as there are family members, and place them face up around the table and close to the copies of the scriptures.

3. Start playing some music. (The leader can play a tape recorder, hum, or sing.) While the music is playing, family members should walk or march around the table. When the music stops, each family member quickly looks at the card closest to him and searches for the matching scripture. Give a ten-second time limit. (You may want to give the younger children longer than the older ones.)

4. If you want to keep score, give one point to each person who found the correct scripture within the time limit.

5. Start the music again and continue playing as long as you wish.

(This game is played in lesson 7.)

Scripture Picture

1. Get the Key Scripture reference cards (from lesson 5) and place them in a bowl.
2. Have each family member draw a card from the bowl.
3. Allow everyone ten minutes to draw a picture about that scripture.
4. At the end of the ten minutes, each person shows his or her picture to the rest of the family and gives an explanation of the drawing.

Scripture Relay

1. Prepare some clues that will direct family members to the key scriptures. Use the Key Scripture statement cards for this purpose, or make up some clues of your own.

2. Divide the family into two teams. Give one sheet of paper to the team and one pen or pencil to each person on the team.

3. Tell the family that you will give a scripture clue. On the word *go*, the first person on each team should write down the reference to the scripture and then pass it to the next

person on his team. That person looks at it and passes it on if she agrees with it. If she disagrees, she crosses it out and writes the reference that she thinks is correct. The sheet works its way through all of the team members until it reaches the last person. The last person must decide if the reference is correct or not and then find it in the scriptures. Any team that finds the correct scripture will receive one point. A bonus point goes to the first team to find it.

First Alternate Idea. On the word *go,* the first person writes a scripture reference on the sheet of paper. Each person writes down a *different* reference as the paper moves through the team. Each team receives one point for each acceptable reference and one more point if the team finished first. They also receive a bonus point for each acceptable reference the other team did not have.

Second Alternate Idea. For this variation, you will need copies of the scriptures for each person and two sets of Key Scripture cards from lesson 5 (use the Key Scripture picture cards and the Key Scripture statement cards). On the word *go,* the first person on each team takes a card, finds the scripture, puts the card in his or her book, and then passes the stack of cards to the next person. That person does the same thing. Play continues until all the cards are gone. Each team receives a point for each scripture they correctly found and a bonus point if their team finished first.

Three Up

1. Prepare clues that will direct the players to the key scriptures. Use the Key Scripture statement cards for this purpose, or make up your own clues.

2. Give a clue and allow ten or fifteen seconds for members to find the scripture. The first three players to find the scripture should stand up or raise their hands. These three, in turn, tell one thing that the scripture talks about. Everyone who found the scripture in the allotted time gets a point. The first three receive an extra point each if they told about one thing found in the scripture.

(This game is played in lesson 23.)

Games for
Many Occasions

The games in this section are designed to give family members a chance to review gospel concepts in a fun and interesting way. Games and activities stimulate family involvement and can actually make it easier for family members to get serious when they should. When family games and activities are handled properly, not only can learning take place but family relationships can be strengthened.

Use the following games in your family home evenings to reinforce concepts taught in the lessons in this book, or use them in other ways to suit your family's needs and wishes. The games are arranged here in alphabetical order.

Danger

1. The object of the game is to guess the secret word within a ninety-second time limit (two minutes could be given when the clue giver is a younger child).

2. At least twenty secret words need to be selected and written on small pieces of paper. On these same papers (let's call them "word cards") write three words that cannot be used when giving clues. These are companion words that would usually be used in describing the secret word. (For example, if the secret word were *baptism,* the three unmentionable words might be *eight, water,* and *covenants.*) These words are already prepared for lesson 28.

3. Divide the family into two teams and have the team members sit together. Select one person from each team to time the other team and one person to check that the other team doesn't use the unmentionable words. Shuffle the word cards and put them in a bowl or similar container.

4. Team 1 chooses a person on their team who will give the clues. The clue giver goes to the front of the room and draws out one of the word cards. The top word on the card is the secret word and the three words that follow are the words that can't be used. He should show the paper to the person who will check him. When everyone's ready, the timer starts timing the ninety seconds.

5. The clue giver says anything—except the forbidden words—that will help his team quickly guess the secret word. They must guess the exact word, not just a form of it. As soon as they guess correctly, he draws another word and starts giving clues for that one. He continues until the timer calls, "Time." If one secret word seems especially difficult, he may pass and draw a new word. Only one pass is allowed per turn. (Here is an example: The secret word is *baptism.* The clue giver could say things like "Ordinance," or "This is something John did to Jesus," or "This is an ordinance that all of us participate in when we are young." If the team said, "Baptized," the clue giver could say that they had guessed a form of the word and the team would have to continue guessing until the word *baptism* was given.)

6. The game is called "Danger" because it is very easy to slip up and say one of the forbidden words. The clue giver must not use any part or form of the secret word or of the forbidden words. If this happens, the watcher from the other team will call out, "Foul," and

the points for that word go to the other team. The clue giver would then quickly draw another word and start giving clues.

7. When the ninety seconds have expired, the points are totaled up and a player from team 2 will become the clue giver for his team.

8. Continue playing by alternating between teams and giving each person a turn as clue giver. The game is over when you run out of secret words, or time, or players. Be sure both teams have had equal turns.

9. Scoring is as follows: Two points for each word guessed; two points for the other team when the clue giver accidentally says the secret word or one of the forbidden words; two points for the other team if the person giving the clue decides to pass and not play one of the words.

10. Time will usually expire while a team is trying to guess a word. When this happens, the other team has one chance to guess the word. If they guess correctly, they receive the two points. They must give their guess within ten seconds.

(This game is played in lesson 28.)

Dress Up

1. Select at least ten questions from the chapters "Game Questions" and/or "Children's Questions."

2. Locate many fun articles of clothing such as old hats, large dresses, old sweaters and coats, gloves, ties, scarfs, aprons, etc. Have at least five articles of clothing for each team.

3. Divide the family into two or more teams and give them their articles of clothing. Decide whether you will direct the questions to the team as a group or to the individual members.

4. Each team designates a team member to be their model. This person will put on his or her team's articles of clothing when called for during game play.

5. Ask the first team a question. If the answer is correct, there is no penalty and play moves on to the next team and the next question. If the answer is incorrect, the team model has to put on one of the articles of clothing. Then play continues with the next team and next question.

6. The game ends when one of the team models is wearing all of the team's clothing. The winner is the team whose model is wearing the least amount of that team's clothing.

7. If desired, begin again by removing the extra clothes, choosing new models, and asking more questions.

"Get the Picture?"

1. Draw a picture on one side of a piece of paper. On the back of the picture, draw puzzle pieces. (The puzzle is already made for lesson 26.)

2. Write a scripture reference and a question on the blank side of each of the puzzle pieces.

3. Run off enough copies of the picture-puzzle for each team.

4. Cut each copy of the puzzle into individual puzzle pieces and place the sets of pieces for each puzzle in separate envelopes.

5. Give each team one of the envelopes containing the puzzle pieces. On the word *go,* each team takes *one* puzzle piece from their envelope, looks up the scripture, and writes the answer to the question on the back of the puzzle piece. One member quickly runs to the person conducting the game and shows him their answer.

6. If their answer is correct, they take the puzzle piece back to the team and lay it face

up on a flat surface so that they can start putting together the puzzle. They then take out another piece of the puzzle.

7. Teams continue to answer their questions and put their puzzles together until all of the teams have completed their puzzles. Younger children can be working on putting the puzzle pieces together while older family members respond to the question on the next puzzle piece.

8. The team to complete their puzzle first is the winner, but everyone will learn something and have a good time.

Golfo

1. Obtain sixteen paper cups and write the numerals 1 through 16 on the inside of the cups. (Pieces of tape can be placed in the cups to write on if necessary.)

2. Place a piece of masking tape on the floor at one end of the room. It needs to be long enough that the cups can be lined up along the tape with about an inch between each cup. Make sure that the cups are mixed up so that the numbers are in random order. The cups are placed on the line, open end down so no one can see the numbers.

3. Get pen or pencils for each person. Use the grids from lesson 30 or draw game grids with sixteen squares (four rows down and four across). Make enough game grids for each family member to have one. Have each player write the sixteen numbers into the squares in random order. Each player will now have a game grid that is unlike any other.

4. Obtain enough grid markers for each player, allowing ten to fifteen per person. Buttons, coins, popcorn, or paper cutouts could be used. Give each player a set.

5. Obtain a putter and a golf ball or substitute. If a larger ball is used, the gap between the cups may need to be increased so that only one cup is hit at a time.

6. Divide the family into two teams. Choose one person from each team to keep track of the team score.

7. A person from the first team putts the ball (or rolls it) and tries to hit one of the cups. When he hits one hard enough that it slides off the tape or falls over, read aloud the number in the cup. The putting team scores the number of points shown in the cup, and each person on both teams places a marker on that number on his game grid. The cup is then removed from the game.

8. A player from the second team putts at the cups and play continues as described.

9. When someone gets four markers in a row on his grid, he is declared the top Golfo player. However, continue playing until every player has four in a row on his grid. As soon as everyone has four in a row, the game ends and the team with the most points is considered the winner. The cups can be reset and another game played if desired.

Alternate Idea. Questions can be included in the game if desired. If using questions, a team would have to answer a question correctly in order to putt the ball. The questions could be taken from the chapters titled "Game Questions" and "Children's Questions."

High-Low

1. Use this activity to learn or review things that have order to them, such as the Presidents of the Church, events in Church history, etc.

2. Select one peron as the thinker. He or she thinks of a person, event, or thing to be guessed (for example, Wilford Woodruff, or the appearance of Moroni to Joseph Smith). The thinker tells the rest of the family what the category is (such as "Presidents of the Church").

3. Family members take turns guessing what the person is thinking. For each guess,

the thinker tells if the guess is high (comes after the correct answer) or low (comes before the correct answer).

4. Continue this process until the correct answer is given.

Alternate Idea. Divide the family into teams and have the teams take turns guessing. (This game is played in lessons 5, 21, and 23.)

Hoops

1. Prepare a list of fifteen to twenty gospel questions. These may be selected from the "Game Questions" chapter or "Children's Questions" chapter.

2. Set a wastebasket, bucket, or other large container at one end of the room. Place five pieces of masking tape on the floor at progressive distances from the basket, such as two, four, six, eight, and ten feet.

3. Find a ball or substitute that will fit into the container. You could use a beanbag or a Nerf ball, or a tape ball made by wadding up several pieces of paper and wrapping masking tape around them.

4. Divide the family into two teams and decide which team goes first.

5. Ask the first team a gospel question. If they answer it correctly, their team scores two points and has an opportunity to shoot for additional points. If the question is answered incorrectly, no points are received, and play rotates to the other team.

6. When the question is answered correctly, one of the team members decides which point line to shoot from. He then attempts to shoot the ball into the basket. If he misses, the team receives no additional points. If he makes it, the team receives points based on where the shot was taken. (Younger children can shoot closer or receive twice as many points for making baskets.)

7. The opposing team then takes a turn at answering a question. Continue play, alternating teams. Make sure each family member gets a chance to shoot the ball.

8. End the game when everyone has had a turn to shoot or when one team reaches some predetermined number of points. Another game can then be played if desired.

(This game is played in lesson 29.)

Name That President

1. Get the Presidents of the Church fact cards (introduced in lesson 15). Place them face down in a stack.

2. Divide the family into two or more teams and choose a reader from each team.

3. Explain that a reader will read facts about the Presidents of the Church. The teams should decide in advance how many words they will need to hear in order to identify the President. The team with the lowest bid gets to play, *but* if they cannot give the correct answer by the time the right number of words have been read, the point goes to the other team.

4. Play begins by having the teams bargain back and forth about how many words they need to hear from the fact card in order to identify which President it is. (Example: "We can identify him after we hear eight words.") The team with the lowest bid wins the chance to play.

5. The reader from the other team then draws one of the cards and reads the stipulated number of words from any one of the facts.

6. If the team correctly identifies the President, they receive a point. If they guess incorrectly, the other team receives a point.

7. Teams then bid on the next card, and play continues.

Alternate Idea. Have just one member of the team play in each round, starting with the youngest. This gives everyone a better chance to participate and learn.

Name That Price

1. Obtain the prices from local stores of products you desire to use in the game. (Some products and their prices have been included in lesson 14, where this game is first played.)

2. Write the prices of the products on separate index cards or on individual squares of paper and lay them face down where the family will be able to see them.

3. Write the names of the products (you can draw pictures as well) on separate cards or pieces of paper and place them on top of the prices that they match. (The playing pieces for this game have been included in lesson 14.)

4. Have paper and pencil ready—one sheet to record guesses and one to keep score.

5. Divide the family into several teams based on the size of the family. You only need two players on a team, but each team could consist of several people. (The more teams there are, the more fun it is, but limit the number of teams to five.)

6. Have the team who is guessing first choose the product that will be used during that round.

7. Describe in some detail the product that has been chosen and have team 1 say what they think the retail cost of the product is. Record their answer and then receive and record the answer from team 2. Continue until all of the teams have given their guesses. Write down the team number along with each guess so you can identify each team's answer. The team to guess nearest to the retail cost, without going over the cost of the product, receives the most points.

8. Each team receives points based on how close they were to the price of the product *without going over it*. The team whose guess is closest to the actual cost of the product, without exceeding the item's cost, would receive the most points (five, if there are five teams; four, if there are four teams; etc.). The second to the nearest would receive one point less. Those who exceed the cost of the item receive the fewest points. (Say, for example, the retail cost of the item was $16.95 and five teams guessed $12.50, $13.95, $13.98, $16.99, and $17.25. The guess of $13.98 would receive five points because it was nearest to $16.95 without going over. $13.95 and $12.50 would receive four points and three points, respectively. Since the guesses of $16.99 and $17.25 both exceed the cost of the item, those teams receive the fewest points. The team guessing $16.99 receives two points and the one guessing $17.25 receives one point.)

9. Since it is an advantage to be last, a different team should start the guessing on each new product. This will ensure equal opportunities for each team.

10. When all of the products have been used, the team with the most points is declared the winner.

(This game is played in lesson 14.)

Numbered Chairs

1. Prepare a list of twenty gospel questions that can be answered in one, two, or three words. You can select some from "Game Questions" or "Children's Questions."

2. Write the answers on slips of paper, one complete set of answers per team and one answer per slip (see the answer slips at the end of the lesson 12 prepared for that lesson). Place each set of answers in separate envelopes.

3. Divide the family into four teams and give a set of answers to each team (a larger group would use more questions and be divided into more teams; a smaller group would have two teams).

4. Each team distributes the answer slips as evenly as possible among the team members. Teams do not need the same number of players but it should be as equal as possible. Four different people, one on each team, will have the same answer.

5. Place four chairs facing into the room. Write the numbers 1, 2, 3, and 4 on separate pieces of paper and tape them on the front side of the chair backrests. Family members sit at the other end of the room and should be able to see the numbers. Each chair is worth one, two, three, or four points.

6. Each player lays his answer slips face up in front of him so that he can see each answer.

7. Explain that when you read a question, everyone should look among his slips for the answer. If they find a correct answer, they should pick up the corresponding slip, run to the opposite end of the room, and sit in the highest numbered chair available. If the answers are correct, they will receive points corresponding to the numbers on the chairs they sit in. If an answer is incorrect, the points are lost.

8. Occasionally two players from the same team will run up and sit in the chairs. Once a person is seated he cannot change chairs or return to his seat. If this happens, both plus and minus points will be received corresponding with the chairs they were in. Since they took a chair that belonged to another team, the team that did not get a chair will receive points based on the chair that the person with the wrong answer sat in.

9. Begin play by reading the first question.

10. Stop playing after ten questions. The team with the most points wins. Then start again with the remaining questions. This gives teams who are behind a chance to start fresh. Keep score as you go along. The answer slips will not be used twice so they can be returned to the envelopes as they are used. Save the envelopes so the game can be played some other time.

(This game is played in lesson 12.)

Plates and Wagons

1. Prepare a list of at least fifteen gospel questions. You can select them from "Game Questions" or "Children's Questions."

2. Remove numbers 1 through 15 from the numbered squares envelope and lay them on the table or floor in a horizontal row.

3. The object of the game is to get three gold plates or three covered wagons in a row (the game pieces are found in lesson 20).

4. Divide the family into two teams. Give the wagons to team 1 and the gold plates to the other team.

5. Ask team 1 a question. If they answer it correctly, they place one wagon over one of the fifteen numbers.

6. Ask team 2 a question and continue until one team gets three of their playing pieces in a row (three wagons or three gold plates). Sometimes players will have to decide whether to block the other team or go for the win themselves.

7. If three in a row is obtained easily, the next game could be changed to four in a row. A team would have to get four wagons or plates in a row in order to win.

8. If no team gets the desired number in a row before all of the numbers are covered, the team with the most wagons or plates in a row is declared the winner.

(This game is played in lesson 20.)

Roll the Dice

1. Prepare a list of ten to twenty gospel questions. You can select from "Game Questions" or "Children's Questions."

2. Obtain a six-sided die. (If you do not have a die, write the numbers one to six on small pieces of paper and place them in a bowl or cup. Each time the instructions indicate the die should be thrown, one of the numbers could be drawn out instead. The number should be replaced before another number is drawn.)

3. Divide the family into teams. The number of teams is not important, but three or four teams is usually more fun than just two. One person on each team should have paper and pencil to keep score for the team.

4. Ask team 1 a question. If they answer it correctly, they throw the die to see how many points they receive. The scorekeeper records the points.

5. Ask team 2 a question and continue as described.

6. Play continues until all of the teams have been asked five questions. The team with the most points is declared the winner and a second game can be played if desired.

Seek and Destroy

1. Prepare a list of at least twenty gospel questions. You may select from "Game Questions" or "Children's Questions."

2. Make a blank grid sheet for each family member consisting of sixty-four squares. (See blank grid sheet below. These sheets are already prepared for lesson 32.)

3. Prepare a master sheet that includes at least four negative things that ought to be eliminated from our lives, and four positive things (the example below was prepared for lesson 32). Notice that the negative things can be written up, down, diagonally, forward, or backward. If you decide to play the game again you can design your own board.

	A B C D E F G H
1	
2	
3	
4	
5	
6	
7	
8	

Master Sheet

	A	B	C	D	E	F	G	H
1			S	G	U	R	D	
2	L	I	E				TITHING	
3				KIND	L		A	
4		L		I			N	
5		A	V	HONESTY			G	
6	PRAYER	E					E	
7	D	T					R	
8		S						

4. Divide the family into two teams and give each family member one of the blank grids. These are used to keep track of their team's hits and misses.

5. Explain that the object of the game is to find the letters on the master grid sheet that make up negative words. There are four bad things (five in the example above) and four good ones. First a team must correctly answer a gospel question. That gives them a chance to "shoot." They shoot by identifying a specific square on the grid, naming the number-letter coordinates. You will tell them whether they've hit a good word, hit a letter from a bad one (also tell them which letter), or missed. If they miss, or if they hit one of the positive things, their turn is over. If they hit one of the negative squares, they can continue shooting until they miss. You will also tell them when they have eliminated something negative. They should record the "hit" information on their blank grids.

6. Ask team 1 a question and play as described. Continue play, alternating teams.

7. Play until all of the negative things have been eliminated. The team with the most points is declared the winner.

8. Scoring is as follows:

Each hit of a negative square = 1 point

Each hit of a good square = −2 points

(This game is played in lesson 32.)

271

Shell Game

The object of the game is to discover which cup (shell) is covering the object by answering questions correctly.

1. Prepare a list of gospel questions. Select from "Game Questions" or "Children's Questions."

2. Place five nontransparent glasses, cups, or empty cans upside down in a row.

3. Divide the family into two teams. While the members of team 1 look the other way, someone on team 2 hides the object under one of the cups. The object can be a popcorn kernel, button, bean, or any small object.

4. Ask a member of team 1 a question from the regular questions or from the children's questions. If he answers the question correctly, he can select one of the shells and turn it over. If the object is under the shell, his team receives one point and play passes to the other team. The cups would then be reset and the object would be hidden by team 1. If the object is not under the shell, a second player on team 1 is asked a question and the same procedure is followed.

5. If a question is missed, no cup can be turned over.

6. If the hidden object is found before three questions are asked, one point is received, and play rotates to team 2. The cups are reset and the object hidden under one of them.

7. Here is the *key rule:* After three questions have been asked, if team 1 has not found the hidden object, they have one free guess. If the object is found, a point is received. If not, team 1 receives no point during their turn. Then play rotates to team 2, who will have the cups reset and follow the same procedure.

8. Play continues as previously explained until each team has had five turns (not five questions) at finding the hidden object. The team who has the most points wins.

(This game is played in lesson 16.)

Square Game

1. Prepare a list of twenty-five gospel questions. You may select them from "Game Questions" or "Children's Questions."

2. Make twenty-five markers and label them: A1, A2, A3, A4, A5, B1, B2, B3, B4, B5, C1, C2, C3, C4, C5, D1, D2, D3, D4, D5, E1, E2, E3, E4, E5. (These markers are already made up for lesson 22.) Place these markers in a bowl or small container so they can be drawn out one at a time.

3. Make enough game grids for each player or team. Each game grid is divided into twenty-five squares. The letters *A, B, C, D,* and *E* are written above the five rows of squares and the numbers *1, 2, 3, 4,* and *5* are written down the left hand side of the squares. This makes it possible to refer to the squares as A1, C4, etc. (Five game grids are located at the end of lesson 22.)

4. Each player or team writes or draws in random order in the grid squares one each of the following items (including the designated points):

Smile	10 pts.	Frown	−10 pts.
Gold Plates	20 pts.	Bomb	−20 pts.
Covered Wagon	30 pts.	Cigar	−30 pts.
Savior	40 pts.	Devil	−40 pts.

5. Players should draw stars in the other seventeen squares. These are worth five points each if the question is answered correctly and a minus five points if the question is answered incorrectly.

6. Read a question and let each player or team write their answer on a piece of paper.

7. Tell the correct answer and draw one of the markers from the container. If a player

272

or team answered the question correctly, and they had a star or one of the positive objects in the chosen square, they would receive the appropriate points. If a negative object is in the square, they do not lose any points, because they answered the question correctly.

8. If a player answers the question incorrectly, the opposite is true. They receive no points if a positive object is in the square and receive the appropriate minus points for a star or one of the negative objects.

9. Play continues by asking another question and drawing another marker out of the container. When all of the markers have been drawn, the person or team with the most points is the winner.

(This game is played in lesson 22.)

Twenty-One

In this game, the goal is to be the team whose score is closest to twenty-one without going over. If a team gets exactly twenty-one, they win and the game is over. Here's how to play:

1. Cut out the forty numbered slips found at the end of lesson 25 and place them into a pan or bowl; there are four of each number from 1 through 10. (Be sure to put these numbers in an envelope marked "Twenty-One" when you are through playing the game.)

2. Divide the family into two or more teams, five being the maximum number of teams.

3. Each team starts with a score of ten, which is recorded under each team's number on a marking board or piece of paper.

4. Team 1 is asked a question. If they answer the question correctly, they earn the right to draw one of the numbered slips out of the container. If they answer the question incorrectly, they may not draw a numbered slip and play moves to the next team.

5. *Before* a team draws a numbered slip, they have to decide whether to take the number themselves or to give it to another team. Since the goal is to get as close to twenty-one as possible, without going over, the team may want to give the number away if their score is already close to twenty-one. They may also desire to give the number to another team whose score is close to twenty-one in the hope of putting that team over twenty-one. If a number puts a team over twenty-one, that team's score goes back to ten, but they are still in the game. (Remember, once a team answers a question correctly and earns the right to draw a number, they have to decide whether to keep the number—as well as which team they are going to give it to if they are *not* going to keep it—before they draw the number and learn what it is.)

6. At the end of a predetermined time (say, fifteen minutes) or after a predetermined number of rounds (say, six rounds), each team is given one more question, and the team whose score is closest to twenty-one is declared the winner. Since it is an advantage to be the last team to play, the order of play for the last round could be randomly determined by throwing dice, thinking of a number between one and fifty, or some other method.

7. Note that if a team reaches twenty-one at any time during the game, they automatically win and a new game begins with everyone starting with a score of ten.

(This game is played in lesson 25.)

Game Questions

The following questions have been taken from the Doctrine and Covenants and Church history lessons in this book. Use the ones that work well for your family and skip the others or rewrite them to meet your needs.

Questions for younger children are found in the next chapter. They are general in nature and cover many areas of the gospel, but they can be used with any of the review games that use questions. Instructions for using the children's questions are included in that chapter.

Lesson 2

1. God did not tell us to just read the scriptures, but he told us to do what? (Study, search, or seek.)

2. Fill in the blanks: "By mine own voice or by the voice of my _____ , it is the _____ ." (Servants, same.)

3. Who was rebaptized because he was first baptized in a bathtub? (Spencer W. Kimball.)

4. Who was the only Church President born outside the United States? (John Taylor.)

Lesson 4

5. How old was Joseph Smith when he received the First Vision? (Fourteen years old.)

6. What book in the Bible did Joseph read that helped him decide what to do? (James.)

7. Who appeared to Joseph in the First Vision? (Heavenly Father and Jesus.)

8. In the First Vision, what church was Joseph told to join? (None of them.)

Lesson 6

9. What are two ways we receive promptings from the Holy Ghost? (In our hearts and in our minds.)

Lesson 8

10. How many years passed between the First Vision and the night Moroni appeared to Joseph in his bedroom? (Three.)

11. What were the stones called that helped Joseph translate the Book of Mormon? (Urim and Thummim.)

12. After his first visit to the hill, how many more times did Joseph meet the angel at the hill? (Four.)

13. What was the name of the hill where the plates were buried? (Cumorah.)

14. Who became the scribe for Joseph and helped him finish the Book of Mormon? (Oliver Cowdery.)

15. Which family gave Joseph a place to stay so he could finish the translation of the Book of Mormon? (Whitmer family.)

16. How many copies of the Book of Mormon were first published? (Five thousand.)

17. What was done to make sure the Book of Mormon manuscript was not lost or stolen while it was being printed? (A copy was made and guards were provided.)

18. Name two things a person must do if he or she desires a witness of the Book of Mormon. (Read it, and pray about it.)

Lesson 10

19. What did God say we can do to come off conquerors over Satan? (Pray always.)

Lesson 12

20. Who restored the Aaronic Priesthood? (John the Baptist.)

21. Who was the first person baptized after the Aaronic Priesthood was restored? (Oliver Cowdery.)

22. Who restored the Melchizedek Priesthood? (Peter, James, and John.)

23. Who are the Peter, James, and John who restored the priesthood? (Chief Apostles of Jesus.)

24. Who was with Joseph Smith when the Aaronic Priesthood was restored and when the Melchizedek Priesthood was restored? (Oliver Cowdery.)

25. Which priesthood has the authority to give the gift of the Holy Ghost? (Melchizedek.)

26. Which priesthood was restored first? (Aaronic.)

27. Was the Church organized before or after the priesthood was restored? (After.)

28. What are two of the three keys held by the Aaronic Priesthood? (Ministering of angels, gospel of repentance, baptism by immersion for remission of sins.)

Lesson 14

29. In section 18 of the Doctrine and Covenants, what did the Lord say would bring us great joy in heaven? (Bringing a soul to him.)

Lesson 16

30. In what year was the Church organized? (1830.)

31. In what month and on which day was the Church organized? (April 6.)

32. Why did six people act as organizers in making the Church a legally accepted organization? (To conform with New York law.)

33. Who, besides Joseph Smith, was sustained as a leader of the Church when the Church was first organized? (Oliver Cowdery.)

34. Which section in the Doctrine and Covenants was received during the meeting in which the Church was organized? (Section 21.)

35. What two important people were baptized on the day the Church was organized? (Parents of Joseph Smith.)

36. Who gave the official name for The Church of Jesus Christ of Latter-day Saints? (The Lord in section 115.)

Lesson 18

37. What ordinance renews our baptismal covenants? (Sacrament.)

38. If we keep the promises we make when we partake of the sacrament, what does God promise us? (That his Spirit will be with us.)

39. What are we to remember when we partake of the bread? (The body of Christ; the Savior's death and resurrection.)

40. What are we to remember when we drink the water during the sacrament? (The blood of Christ; that the Savior suffered so much that he bled for us.)

41. Where was Christ when he shed drops of blood as he suffered for our sins? (Garden of Gethsemane.)

42. What can Christ do for us because he suffered for our sins? (Forgive us when we repent.)

43. What promises do we make when we partake of the sacrament? (Take upon us the name of Jesus Christ, always remember him, and keep his commandments.)

Lesson 20

44. Who was the first official missionary for the restored Church of Jesus Christ? (Samuel Smith.)

45. How was Samuel Smith related to Joseph Smith? (He was Joseph's younger brother.)

46. What important thing concerning the Book of Mormon had Samuel done before he was called as a missionary? (He saw and handled the plates.)

47. What kind of success did Samuel have on the first day of his mission? (No success.)

48. Where did Samuel sleep the first night in the mission field? (Under an apple tree on the hard ground.)

49. What two important Church leaders were eventually converted through a Book of Mormon that Samuel sold during his mission? (Brigham Young and Heber C. Kimball.)

50. Who was Heber C. Kimball's grandson, and why was he important? (Spencer W. Kimball; he was a President of the Church.)

Lesson 22

51. In order to repent, what must a person do besides stop doing things that are wrong? (Turn toward God; start to do what God wants us to do.)

52. What did Jesus do for us so that we can be forgiven? (Suffered for our sins.)

53. God wants us to confess or admit our sins to ourselves. Who else does he want us to confess our sins to? (To God; serious sins should be confessed to the bishop also.)

54. God said that he will not remember our sins if we will do what? (Truly repent by forsaking them and confessing them.)

Lesson 24

55. Which latter-day prophet had a lot of accidents in his childhood and youth? (Wilford Woodruff.)

56. In 1838 God commanded the members of the Quorum of the Twelve Apostles to go to which country on missions? (England.)

57. What happened when a policeman showed up at a meeting, intending to arrest Wilford Woodruff? (The policeman became converted.)

Lesson 25

58. What does it mean to keep ourselves unspotted from the world? (Spots are symbols of sin; to keep ourselves unspotted is to avoid sin.)

59. What commandment specifically promises to help us keep unspotted from the world? (Keeping the Sabbath day holy.)

60. Besides spiritual blessings, what else is promised to those who strive to keep the Sabbath day holy? (Fulness of the earth.)

Lesson 28

61. Which brother of Joseph Smith was killed when Joseph was killed? (Hyrum.)

62. Who was the future President of the Church who was in Carthage Jail with Joseph Smith? (John Taylor.)

63. What is a martyr? (Someone who sacrifices his or her life for the sake of something precious like the gospel.)

64. What stopped a bullet meant for John Taylor and saved his life? (His pocket watch.)

65. Who covered the wounded John Taylor with an old mattress in an attempt to save his life? (Willard Richards.)

Lesson 29

66. What comparison can you make between forgiving others and being bitten by a rattlesnake? (When we are offended it is important to get rid of our bitterness immediately or it will poison our souls just as a rattlesnake bite can poison our bodies.)

67. What should we do if we are having a hard time forgiving someone? (Ask God to help us.)

Lesson 30

68. Who became the second President of the restored Church? (Brigham Young.)

69. What miracle did God perform to show that Brigham Young should follow Joseph Smith as Church President? (Made Brigham Young look and sound like Joseph Smith.)

70. What was the group of men called who held the priesthood keys when Joseph was killed? (Quorum of the Twelve Apostles.)

71. What Church leader tried to take over the Church before Brigham Young could return to Nauvoo? (Sidney Rigdon.)

Lesson 32

72. Joseph organized some special instructional meetings which were first held in a room over his kitchen. What were these meetings called? (School of the Prophets.)

73. What took place in the School of the Prophets that caused Joseph to pray and receive the Word of Wisdom? (Men in the meetings smoked and chewed tobacco.)

74. Who complained to Joseph about the filthiness of the room after these meetings were held? (Joseph's wife.)

75. Which section in the Doctrine and Covenants is called the Word of Wisdom? (Section 89.)

76. What two things make up the soul of man? (Spirit and body.)

77. What word from the scriptures describes how spirits in the spirit world consider the separation from their bodies? (*Bondage.*)

78. The Spirit of God cannot dwell in unholy _____ . (Bodies or temples.)

79. What are the four major don'ts of the Word of Wisdom? (Use of tobacco, alcohol, tea, coffee.)

80. What are two of the three important words in the Word of Wisdom that teach the spirit of this commandment? (*Wholesome, prudence, thanksgiving.*)

81. According to a reported statement from Joseph Smith, what do the words *hot drinks* in the revelation known as the Word of Wisdom refer to? (Tea and coffee.)

Children's Questions

These questions can be used in any of the review games. They do not match particular lessons as do the questions in the chapter "Game Questions." To simplify using both sets of questions, paper clip together the pages between the game questions being used and the children's questions being used. This will make it easy to flip back and forth during the game. Skip or rewrite any questions that you do not feel comfortable with. The correct answers have been printed in *italics.*

Almost all children of any age can play the review games if the following adjustments are made:

1. Very young children can be teamed up with someone older. The older person can talk over the answer with the young child and let the child tell what the answer is. This way younger children can feel part of the game and learn something also.
2. The questions in this chapter have been written for children a little older than those described in paragraph 1 above. You can soon tell if the questions are too easy or hard and can move a child back to a team with someone older, or forward to suggestion 3 below.
3. The questions in this chapter can be adapted to children who are a little older by simply dropping the multiple choice option and just reading the questions and allowing the child to think of the correct answer.
4. As soon as you feel a child is old enough, the "Game Questions" should be used when it is that child's turn. Teenagers and adults, of course, will use the "Game Questions."

1. When we partake of the sacrament, what does the bread represent?
   a. Blood of Jesus　　　　b. ***Body of Jesus***

2. Who suffered for our sins so that we could be forgiven?
   a. ***Jesus***　　　　b. Heavenly Father

3. Jesus is our:
   a. Father　　　　b. ***Brother***

4. When we partake of the sacrament, what does the water represent?
   a. ***Blood of Jesus***　　　　b. Body of Jesus

5. What is the Church organization for women called?
   a. ***Relief Society***　　　　b. Mutual

6. The higher priesthood that men may hold was named after which man?
   a. Abraham　　　　b. ***Melchizedek***

7. What is it called when we pay 10 percent of our income to the Lord?
   a. ***Tithing***　　　　b. Fast offering

8. Our earthly fathers are the fathers of our mortal bodies. Who is the father of our spirits?

    a. **_Heavenly Father_**   b. Jesus

9. Who tries to get us to make the wrong choices?

    a. Holy Ghost   b. **_Devil_**

10. When someone new is put in a Church office, what do we do to sustain that person?

    a. **_Hold up our hands_**   b. Shake the person's hand

11. Who interviews us before we are baptized?

    a. **_Bishop_**   b. Primary teacher

12. What have we all been given that lets us know when we have done something wrong?

    a. Mind   b. **_Conscience_**

13. What good quality should we have in order to say no when our friends want us to do something wrong?

    a. **_Courage_**   b. Repentance

14. We make covenants when we are baptized. Which of the following words has the same meaning as the word *covenant?*

    a. **_Promise_**   b. Blessing

15. When we do the things that are right, what are we being for our friends?

    a. A temptation   b. **_A good example_**

16. What is the first principle of the gospel?

    a. **_Faith in the Lord Jesus Christ_**   b. Obedience

17. What does a person need to do before he or she can be confirmed?

    a. Receive the priesthood   b. **_Be baptized_**

18. When someone calls us names, what are we supposed to do?

    a. Call them names back   b. **_Forgive them_**

19. In order to be a good friend to someone, you should:

    a. Do whatever your friend wants to do   b. **_Refuse to do bad things with your friend_**

20. How many persons are there in the Godhead?

    a. **_Three_**   b. Two

21. Which of the following two things will bring us happiness?

    a. **_Keeping God's commandments_**   b. Breaking God's commandments

22. What are the two men called who call on Church members' homes each month?

    a. Visiting teachers   b. **_Home teachers_**

23. Which of the following two things will help your parents trust you more?
    a. Lying　　　　　　　　　b. **Always telling the truth**

24. What is the book called in which people write the things that happen to them each day?
    a. **Journal**　　　　　　　b. Scriptures

25. Which is the better reason for keeping the commandments?
    a. **Because we love God**　b. Because we have to

26. When Jesus comes to the earth for the second time, there will be a thousand-year period of peace and happiness upon the earth. What is this period called?
    a. Heaven　　　　　　　　b. **Millennium**

27. What is the priesthood blessing called that tells you some of your talents and some blessings you can have if you live right?
    a. **Patriarchal blessing**　b. Bishop's blessing

28. How often should you pray?
    a. **Both morning and night** b. Either morning or night

29. Whom were we with before we were born into this earth life?
    a. **Heavenly Father**　　　b. No one; we didn't exist before this life

30. What is it called when you are on time?
    a. A miracle　　　　　　　b. **Punctuality**

31. If we don't repent of our sins, who will be punished for them?
    a. **We will**　　　　　　　b. Jesus will

32. What do we call the event in which our physical bodies come alive again after we die?
    a. **Resurrection**　　　　b. Birth

33. When we are quiet in church and listen to what is being said, we are being:
    a. Repentant　　　　　　　b. **Reverent**

34. What organization can boys join when they are twelve years old?
    a. Cub Scouts　　　　　　b. **Boy Scouts**

35. What does Heavenly Father want us to study every day?
    a. **The scriptures**　　　　b. The newspaper

36. When you do not want to share with others, you are being:
    a. **Selfish**　　　　　　　b. Generous

37. What can you bear on the first Sunday of each month?
    a. Talk　　　　　　　　　b. **Testimony**

38. What does God want us to do with the money that he blesses us with?
    a. **Share it**　　　　　　b. Spend all of it on ourselves

283

39. Where did Heavenly Father and Jesus first appear to Joseph Smith?
    a. Temple
    b. **Sacred Grove**

40. Which group of people does the Book of Mormon talk about?
    a. **Nephites**
    b. Mormonites

41. What is the first book in the Bible called?
    a. John
    b. **Genesis**

42. Which book is Alma found in?
    a. **The Book of Mormon**
    b. New Testament

43. Jesus walked on the Sea of:
    a. **Galilee**
    b. Salt

44. How many articles of faith are there?
    a. Twelve
    b. **Thirteen**

45. One of the books of scripture is called the Pearl of Great:
    a. **Price**
    b. Things

46. What was the name of Moses' brother?
    a. Luke
    b. **Aaron**

47. What were the names of Nephi's rebellious brothers?
    a. Jacob and Joseph
    b. **Laman and Lemuel**

48. Jesus called himself the Good Shepherd, and we are the:
    a. **Sheep**
    b. Cows

49. One way Jesus taught the people was by using stories that were called:
    a. Poems
    b. **Parables**

50. What is sometimes called the still small voice?
    a. **The Holy Ghost**
    b. A whisper

51. What was the occupation of Jesus' stepfather, Joseph?
    a. Fisherman
    b. **Carpenter**

52. Where do we find the Ten Commandments?
    a. New Testament
    b. **Old Testament**

53. From whom did Nephi and his brothers try to get the brass plates?
    a. **Laban**
    b. Ishmael

54. Who created the earth under Heavenly Father's direction?
    a. Noah
    b. **Jesus**

55. Jesus commanded the Nephites to pray in whose name?
    a. **His name**
    b. John the Baptist's

56. How many apostles did Jesus have?
    a. **Twelve**   b. Eleven

57. What man did Jesus raise from the dead?
    a. Luke   b. **Lazarus**

58. What sea did part for Moses and the children of Israel?
    a. The Dead Sea   b. **The Red Sea**

59. What sea did Jesus calm?
    a. The Dead Sea   b. **The Sea of Galilee**

60. How many days was Jonah in the belly of the fish?
    a. **Three**   b. Five

61. Who tried walking on the water after Jesus?
    a. Luke   b. **Peter**

62. What is the name of Joseph Smith's older brother who was killed with him?
    a. William   b. **Hyrum**

63. Who was Jesus Christ's chief Apostle?
    a. Luke   b. **Peter**

64. In what city did Joseph and Mary look for Jesus for three days?
    a. **Jerusalem**   b. Bethlehem

65. What was the instrument called that guided Lehi and his family in the wilderness?
    a. **Liahona**   b. Map

66. What was the name of Lehi's wife?
    a. Emma   b. **Sariah**

67. What prophet in the Book of Mormon was burned to death?
    a. Nephi   b. **Abinadi**

68. Who knows what you are thinking besides you?
    a. **Heavenly Father**   b. Satan

69. Who came to Jesus while he was in the wilderness?
    a. **Satan**   b. Mary

70. What is the name of the angel who gave Joseph Smith the gold plates?
    a. **Moroni**   b. Gabriel

71. What was the name of the Lamanite prophet who came to the Nephites five years before Jesus was born?
    a. Alma   b. **Samuel**

72. What animal did Samson slay with his bare hands?
    a. A bear   b. **A lion**

73. What sign did the Lord give Noah to show that He promised never to destroy the earth by flood again?
   a. **A rainbow**
   b. A cloud

74. Who followed Joseph Smith and became the second President of the Church?
   a. Ezra Taft Benson
   b. **Brigham Young**

75. What two meetings do fathers attend while their children are in Primary?
   a. **Sunday School and priesthood meeting**
   b. Sunday School and Relief Society

76. How much tithing should be paid on one dollar?
   a. **Ten cents**
   b. One cent

77. What city was Jesus born in?
   a. **Bethlehem**
   b. Nazareth

78. What Primary class has a class ring?
   a. The Blazer class
   b. **The CTR class**

79. What was described as "two stones in silver bows . . . fastened to a breastplate"?
   a. The golden plates
   b. **Urim and Thummim**

80. What is the fast offering money used for?
   a. To build churches
   b. **To help needy people**

81. All but one of the Articles of Faith begin with what two words?
   a. **We believe**
   b. Thou shalt

82. In what general way did the Lamanites look different from the Nephites?
   a. The Lamanites had angry faces
   b. **The Lamanites had dark skin**

83. What holiday celebrates the resurrection of Jesus?
   a. Christmas
   b. **Easter**

84. How much of the earth was covered with water when it rained during the great flood?
   a. **The whole earth**
   b. Half of the earth

85. What name did the angel Gabriel tell Zacharias to give his son?
   a. **John**
   b. Moses

86. What ward leaders conduct sacrament meeting?
   a. The stake presidency
   b. **The bishop and his counselors**

87. Who told Mary that her cousin Elisabeth was going to have a baby?
   a. **Angel Gabriel**
   b. Angel Moroni

88. What did Adam and Eve use to make aprons for themselves?
   a. Grape leaves
   b. **Fig leaves**

89. Which Apostle betrayed Jesus?
    a. Peter   b. **_Judas Iscariot_**

90. Ether was the last prophet of what group of people?
    a. Nephites   b. **_Jaredites_**

91. The two men named Alma in the Book of Mormon are what relation to each other?
    a. **_Father and son_**   b. Brothers

92. During the time of Christ, anyone who was not a Jew was called a what?
    a. Mormon   b. **_Gentile_**

93. The three degrees of glory are the telestial, the terrestrial, and the _____ kingdoms.
    a. **_Celestial_**   b. Zion

94. Jesus taught his disciples to pray by demonstrating with a special prayer. What has this prayer come to be called?
    a. **_The Lord's Prayer_**   b. The Beginning Prayer

95. Who was the last survivor of the Nephites?
    a. Ether   b. **_Moroni_**

96. What two things carried the pioneers' belongings on the trek across the plains?
    a. **_Handcarts and covered wagons_**   b. Railcars and barges

97. Where are celestial marriages performed?
    a. In the chapel   b. **_In the temple_**

98. What is the name of the youngest Primary class?
    a. Stars   b. **_Sunbeams_**

99. Which of the books of scripture has a dictionary in it?
    a. Book of Mormon   b. **_Bible_**

100. What did the Anti-Nephi-Lehies do with their weapons?
    a. **_They buried them_**   b. They used them against their enemies